THE GREAT INDEX MANIA

The Stock Market (1997 - 2002)

By Jeffrey B. Little

LIBERTY PUBLISHING COMPANY
Deerfield Beach, Florida

Published by:

Liberty Publishing Company, Inc.
440 South Federal Highway, Suite 202
Deerfield Beach, Florida 33441

http://www.libertypub.com

ISBN 0-89709-216-3

The charts appearing in this book are reprinted with permission
of the copyright owner M.C. Horsey & Company, Inc. of
Salisbury, Maryland. (410) 742-3700

The cartoon (page 119) is courtesy of Jeff MacNelly.
Visit his website at http://www.macnelly.com

Manufactured USA

To Judy

Publisher's Preface

The Great Index Mania was originally scheduled for publication in late 1998. However, events seem to be unfolding far more rapidly than we imagined several months ago forcing us to move its schedule ahead. Also, it goes without saying that this book now has a very broad audience with a greater need for this information than ever before.

A subtitle, "How to Avoid the Next Stock Market Crash" would be more provocative than the present one, we admit. But it was titled as such because it is *not* our intention to introduce this book as just another "sensationalist" effort. Even though that message will be the area of greatest interest for most readers, we expect this text to soon be acknowledged as *the* reference on bear markets and crashes for years to come.

The Great Index Mania has three primary objectives: First, to explain why a crash is likely to occur; second, to help the reader anticipate and identify the point when it offers the greatest investment risk; and third, to help the reader make the most of a potentially bad situation. Today, there are over 60 million investors -- millions of whom are risking, unknowingly, a huge portion of their financial well-being.

Stock market circumstances change rapidly, and the situation might be completely different when you read this book than when it was written. However, considering the conditions at the time of its publication, when you finally put this book down, it's very likely your primary question won't be IF, but WHEN?

Liberty Publishing Company

Table of Contents

Introduction

For the past thirty years, most of the people participating in the stock market can be generally divided into two groups...

Those who trade short term and typically buy shares of stock with a willingness and a discipline to exit immediately if the price moves opposite original expectations. They adhere to an old Wall Street adage, "buy low, and cut your losses quickly."

Then there are those who invest with a longer term horizon. They are disciples of some of the most successful Wall Street advisors and money managers such as the late T. Rowe Price, and John Templeton, and Warren Buffet, all of whom have been known to say, in so many words, "It's better to invest for the long pull, be patient, stay the course, and don't attempt to play the short term market swings." In other words, "buy good stocks and hold them because it's impossible to consistently BUY LOW and SELL HIGH."

As history clearly demonstrates, this investment approach is a proven one. It has worked well for countless investors for many decades, or longer. However, in some respects, the success of this approach, especially in recent years, is the underlying reason for today's enormous and serious problem.

The mutual fund has become the investment darling of the so-called "baby-boomer" generation. Nothing could be sweeter. To a busy executive or a hard working wage-earner, the mutual fund is a common-sense answer to the dilemma, "How can I invest for the long term, and do it properly, when buying the right stocks requires analysis and a slice of time that I don't have?"

The fact that a greater number of mutual funds exists today than there are companies available for investment speaks volumes about the financial arena. An entire generation is now investing in the stock market through the "professional management" of IRA and 401(k) plans. Money is deducted regularly from paychecks or deposited religiously into investment accounts, tax-deferred, leaving the mutual fund analysts and managers to do the necessary research and stock selection.

There is now a major problem with this picture, and this book will explain why a stock market collapse is becoming more certain by the day. Never before has so much personal wealth been riding on a rise or a decline of the stock market, including the boom years leading to the stock market crash in late 1929! This book will also serve as a practical guide to help the reader anticipate, and perhaps even profit from, a debacle that will almost certainly affect us all for years to come.

Jeff Little

CHAPTER ONE
MANIAS AND CRASHES

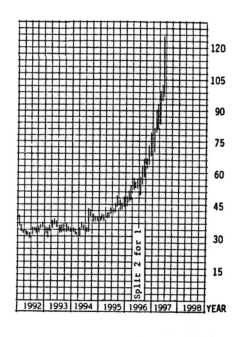

Manias and Crashes

When the tulip was first introduced into Europe from Turkey sometime after 1550, this colorful flower gained such popularity that, by 1635, personal fortunes in Holland were being made and lost overnight with the price swings of these long-stemmed beauties. This was a time when a suit of clothes could have been purchased for approximately 100 florins — only a small fraction of the record price commanded for a single Semper Augustus bulb at more than 5,100 florins.

In 1637, within just a few months, the prices for most varieties of tulips plunged to only 10%, or less, of their prior quotes and the legend of the "Tulip Mania" was born. It then became the perfect example of people losing sight of reality as they chased false hopes of easy gains.

Many of the same lessons can be drawn from the rapid rise and fall of The Mississippi Scheme during the 1717-1720 period. At that time, John Law's Compagnie d'Occident obtained exclusive rights to develop the French Mississippi Valley territories and a great segment of the population in France participated in the initial success and downfall of the venture.

The South-Sea Bubble in England during the 1719-1720 period had a similar story line. The South-Sea Company had been granted exclusive trading rights to the South Seas. When the price of the shares rose from 128 1/2 to 1000 in about eight months, many citizens enjoyed instant wealth and used their high-quality South-Sea shares as collateral for other business ventures. Once the population learned that the Company Chairman and a few others had quietly sold their stock, the price returned to under 130 in just a matter of weeks.

1929

On October 17, 1929, Professor Irving Fisher of Yale made one of the most incredible statements ever when he said: "Stocks have reached what looks like a permanently high plateau." This was a particularly noteworthy comment considering that just twenty-two years before, and within the memory of most investors on that day, J.P. Morgan, almost singlehandedly, took action to end the Panic of 1907. Moreover, the plunge of nearly 50% between 1919 and 1921 seemed all but forgotten. On Wall Street, as we now realize, once new investors enter this exciting arena, memories of past debacles tend be shorter.

The relentless advance of stock values between June, 1924 and late 1925 gathered renewed momentum in early 1927. It continued into the Fall of 1929. During that time, investor "pools" were being formed to trade stocks. Perhaps most famous was the RCA pool headed by broker/specialist Michael J. Meehan. Every day investors would be searching the financial news asking "What's Meehan, Durant, or Jesse Livermore doing today?"

The rise and fall of "blue chip" stocks during the late stages of this period was extraordinary. U.S. Steel, for example, began the year 1929 near $160 per share and reached an all-time high of $261 3/4 in early September. The stock market crash encompassed a two-day period (Monday, October 28th, and Tuesday, the 29th). The crash took "Steel" as low as $166 1/2 on Tuesday morning, down about 36% from its high just a few weeks earlier.

Stockholders were shocked to see it below its $203 "book value." About one-third of the initial drop was recovered with a rally that continued into early 1930. Then the slide resumed. In June, 1932, the stock's decline finally ended at $22 per share. U.S. Steel didn't return to its 1929 high until May, 1955.

1972

Tuesday, November 14, 1972 marked the first time in history that the Dow Jones Industrial Average closed above 1000. Almost exactly twenty-five months later, on December 9, 1974, the Dow Jones Industrial Average touched 570.01, ending the most painful bear market since the 1930's and marking the start of the most powerful bull market in the entire history of Wall Street.

But there was a 4 1/2 year cycle between May, 1970 and December, 1974 that people will never forget. It was appropriately dubbed "The Nifty-Fifty Era," and it produced one of the wildest rides investors ever experienced with major equity holdings.

The drop of more than 46% of the popular market averages was modest when compared to the damages inflicted on porfolios by many of the Nifty-Fifty favorites. And they moved in concert, almost to the day. Xerox rose from $66 to $171, and declined to $50. Avon Products went from $60, up to $140, and down to $19. IBM climbed from $178, to $364, and down to $151; Polaroid, $51, up to $149, and then down to almost $14. And Coca Cola rose from $64 to $150, then down to $44. As a group, these five stocks rose an average of 144% to their 1972 peaks and then dropped an average of 76% to their lows in 1974!

These were *quality* companies, representing a great many "core" growth stock holdings of the day. Each had it's own private "crash." During the fourth quarter of 1973, Avon lost 41% of its value and Polaroid shed 48%. During the third quarter of 1974, Xerox lost 46%, IBM 33%, and Coca Cola 56%.

What were investors thinking when they accumulated shares at such prices? At its peak in 1972, Xerox was valued at 45 times *projected* 1973 earnings per share; Avon at 60 times; IBM at 34 times; Polaroid at 94 times; and Coca Cola at 42 times! And three of the five (Avon, Polaroid, and Coca Cola) struggled to earn as much in 1974 as they did in 1972! Not only were they overpriced, but earnings growth failed to meet expectations. In fact, one rationalization for a rich P/E multiple in the first place is a "high visability" of projected profits.

There's a benefit of owning shares of quality companies. With some patience, they can recover; although holders in 1929 had to wait about twenty-five years. Of the five growth stocks mentioned here, IBM was the first to surpass its 1972-73 high (in December, 1982), followed by Coca Cola (November, 1985), and then came Xerox (September, 1996). Unfortunately, Polaroid and Avon shareholders had to wait twenty-five years.

1987

When the word "crash" is mentioned on Wall Street, typically the reference is to either October, 1929, or to October, 1987. It's interesting to note that the technical similarities between the two events are striking, as a later chapter illustrates.

However, unlike 1929, the economy in 1987 was not facing anything close to the difficulties experienced fifty-eight years earlier. Excessive valuations were corrected with an emotional plunge, but reason prevailed, and those with a longer term investment horizon, provided they had the capital, used the crash to their advantage.

Clearly, U.S. equities were at excessive levels in 1987, just as they had been in 1962, and again in 1972, when stock prices plunged 30% and 46%, respectively. But in 1987, as in both earlier periods, corporate profits were headed higher in the two years that followed.

Comparing the two crash scenarios, 1929 and 1987, can be very instructive (see Chapter 4). In 1929, the Dow Jones Industrial Average reached a peak on September 3rd at 386.10 and crashed eight weeks later to a low of

212.33, a 45% drop. In 1987, the DJIA peaked on August 25th at 2747 and also crashed eight weeks later to a low of 1616, a 41% decline. In each case, prices at the top were approximately twice the level attained twenty-four months earlier. Obviously, these were not unlike most other bull markets — a great many investors were sitting on substantial profits.

By August, 1987 investors found it easy to reminisce about stocks of just three, four, or five years earlier. It was not uncommon to find shares of well-known companies that had advanced 300%, or 400%, and sometimes substantially more.

Many "old timers" had uneasy feelings by mid-1987 when dramatic, personal experiences were being repeated almost before their very eyes. One case in point was Brunswick Corporation.

During the late 1950's, Brunswick, the manufacturer of bowling equipment and other leisure-time products, entered a period of substantial growth. Earnings per share rose from $0.69 in 1957, to $1.07 in 1958; $1.71 in 1959; $2.28 in 1960; and to $2.56 per share in 1961. Reflecting this growth, "BC" advanced from a split-adjusted $3 per share in early 1957 to more than $74 in March, 1961. The stock, as they say, "went parabolic" when its price accelerated as if it were a rocket to the moon.

For Brunswick, history seemed to be repeating in 1987. The company's earnings per share entered a growth phase in much the same way it did 26 years earlier. In 1983, earnings per share were reported to be $0.73, and climbed to $1.10 in 1984; $1.17 in 1985; $1.31 in 1986; and to $1.90 in 1987. Meanwhile, the split-adjusted shares of the now-larger company rose in a similar parabolic manner from $3 in early 1983 to about $30 by August, 1987.

BRUNSWICK CORPORATION

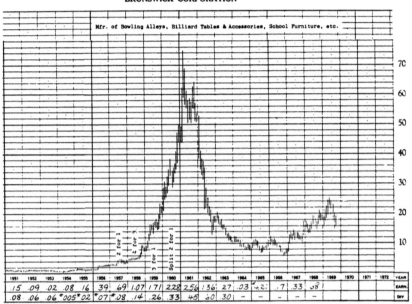

Mfr. of Bowling Alleys, Billiard Tables & Accessories, School Furniture, etc.

YEAR	1951	1952	1953	1954	1955	1956	1957	1958	1959	1960	1961	1962	1963	1964	1965	1966	1967	1968	1969	1970	1971	1972
EARN.	.15	.09	.02	.08	16	39	69	1.07	171	228	256	136	27	.03	+2	.7	.33	38				
DIV	.08	.06	.06	*.005	*.02	*.07	*.08	.14	.26	.33	45	60	30	–	–	–	–	–	–			

BRUNSWICK CORPORATION

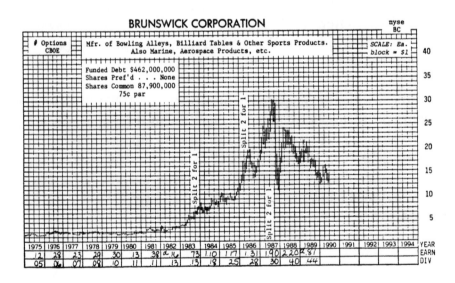

nyse
BC

Options
CBOE

Mfr. of Bowling Alleys, Billiard Tables & Other Sports Products.
Also Marine, Aerospace Products, etc.

SCALE: Ea.
block = $1

Funded Debt $462,000,000
Shares Pref'd . . . None
Shares Common 87,900,000
75¢ par

YEAR	1975	1976	1977	1978	1979	1980	1981	1982	1983	1984	1985	1986	1987	1988	1989	1990	1991	1992	1993	1994
EARN	12	28	23	29	30	13	38	2.16	73	1.10	117	131	190	220	81					
DIV	05	06	07	08	10	11	11	13	13	18	25	28	30	40	44					

In less than five years, Hershey Foods shares climbed 500% from the split-adjusted price of $6 per share to $37, while earnings per share increased at a rate of roughly 15% annually over the same period. It was almost as if the ubiquitous Hershey bar, attained a new status, greater than ever before.

In October, as prices were sliding, and exactly ten days before they crashed, one market writer made this observation: "Market timers are like the girl with the little curl right in the middle of her forehead. When they're good, they're very, very good; and when they're bad, they're just horrible." And in that same article, it was said: "Overall, the results (of a recent Calgary study) showed that it is more important to correctly forecast bull markets than bear markets." Unfortunately, it was not mentioned in the article that IBM, which closed at $147 3/8 that day, would not see that price for another nine years.

Mutual Funds were very much on the scene in 1987. The funds continued to buy shares at ever-increasing prices throughout the first half of 1987. Also at this time, new funds were being created that had been authorized to use stock options and stock index futures to hedge against losses in the stock and bond markets. As Summer approached, despite their higher operating costs, funds of this type were achieving quarterly gains well above the single-digit increases enjoyed by the popular market averages. Whenever they called the short-term market swings correctly, profits from futures trading would swell, even though potential gains are normally limited with hedging activity. Once the stock market crashed, however, investors discovered that these funds can also drop sharply in value.

Since the 1987 crash, the Securities and Exchange Commission (SEC) and the New York Stock Exchange have imposed "curbs" and "collars" on trading activity. Today, when the Dow advances or declines by 50 or more points, trading curbs are imposed, limiting the activity of computer-generated trading (designed to take advantage of the disparity between futures prices and the respective "cash" values of those stocks).

In addition, the single-day, 508-point drop on October 19 led to the creation of "collars" which, in effect, allow investors and traders to "catch their breath." At this writing, these collars have never been used. However, with the ever-increasing volatility, it is reasonable to assume that they will most likely be called upon within the next year or so.

If the Dow Jones Industrial Average advances or declines by 350 points, trading on the New York Stock Exchange (presumably to be followed by the other exchanges) will be stopped for 30 minutes. If, after trading resumes, the market extends its move another 200 points, then a two-hour halt will be put into effect. One experienced trader expressed frustration with the idea by saying: "Yeah, this will provide an opportunity for me to contemplate my navel and to calculate my potential losses more accurately."

Will the collars prove effective? The answer isn't clear. Yet it is easy to imagine how they might add to the emotional swings of the day, especially if the direction is down. One possibility might be an early shutdown, followed by a re-opening "gap-up" as investors scramble to catch the lows and, for just a moment, try to re-live the great opportunities presented to them on October 20, 1987.

CHAPTER TWO
THE GREAT INDEX MANIA

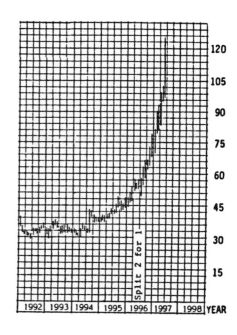

The Great Index Mania

There's an old Wall Street saying: "The stock market is motivated by two emotions, greed and fear." And this is certainly true when the term "mania" is applied, whether the subject is stocks, tulips, art, real estate, stamps, or even a collection of beer cans. However, for the sake of simplicity, let us apply the term "mania" to a stock market in which prices are rising "simply because they are rising." This definition, in turn, implies that stock prices are being accepted freely, without regard for historic valuation guidelines, or any realistic assessment of potential investment returns, again, using history as a guide.

Back in the late 1960's, attention was drawn to high-profile managers such as Gerry Tsai who attracted large sums of money to his newly-created Manhattan Fund. During these "early days" of performance, portfolio managers would monitor the day-to-day activities and the relative ratings of Fidelity, Dreyfus, and several others, and compare themselves, almost daily, to this "fierce competition."

The constant and unrelenting drive for performance in recent years has made life especially difficult for today's mutual fund portfolio managers. They've also found it necessary to adapt to several important changes affecting their industry since those early days. First, a much larger segment of the industry is "no-load," which represents lower costs to today's investor, plus a greater freedom to shift money from one fund to another. Second, many funds are now members of a "family" of mutual funds with each offering a different objective. Thus, investors can switch from one fund to another within the family, often with only one phone call. Third, the retirement savings of the so-called "baby-boomer" generation can be found in IRA and 401(k) plans managed for the investors through these funds.

Finally, and most important, portfolio managers and fund holders are now comparing their fund's performance (not just annually, but quarterly, and even monthly) to a popular, broad market average called the Standard & Poor's 500. This is nothing new. The S&P 500 Index has been an excellent benchmark of comparison since it was first calculated in 1957. However, something new *has* been added to the landscape: the Index Fund.

Weighted according to the market value of each security in it, the S&P 500 Index accounts for more than 80% of the dollar market value of all stocks listed on the New York Stock Exchange. Today, General Electric, also one of the 30 stocks in the Dow Jones Industrial Average, has the largest market capitalization (now close to $250 billion) of all U.S. equities. Although the rankings will change, of course, of the twenty largest "big-cap" equities in the U.S., twelve are in the Dow Jones Industrial Average which explains why the DJIA and the S&P 500 have advanced and declined almost in lock-step over the years.

So, what's the problem?

Over the past several years, the vast majority of professional portfolio managers have failed to match the performance of the Standard & Poor's 500. In fact, in 9 of the past 15 years, at least 75% of the portfolio managers have been unable to beat this simple index! So now, each new day, fund holders are asking themselves: "Hey, if my professional manager can't beat the S&P 500, why should I be investing my money in *that* fund? Why not buy shares in the benchmark they haven't been able to beat?" And who can blame them? Both the S&P 500 and the Dow Industrials are representative of some of the best-managed, highest-quality companies in the world!

In 1994, index funds accounted for only $23 billion, which was then a small slice of the entire mutual fund industry. Today, this select group accounts for well over $100 billion and it is rising steadily, with new index funds still being created. This is still a relatively small slice of the industry, with Vanguard Group being the largest. However, now, index funds are only a "tip of the iceberg" because, to match the performance or to avoid falling behind, portfolio managers have found it necessary, almost regardless of their charters, to add the same names to their portfolios. It isn't clear how many "pseudo" index funds exist, but the total number is not small.

Here is a typical example of how assets have been shifting over the past few years. This is a small/medium-sized fund with INCOME as an objective. It will remain nameless here. Found among its eight largest holdings, in order of size: American Express, IBM, Bristol Myers, Procter & Gamble, and General Electric. Among the stocks bought recently: IBM, Microsoft, Coca Cola, Avon Products, and Intel. Among those sold recently: Monsanto, Salomon Inc., Bell South, Ford Motor, and Mobil. The five mentioned among the largest had an average dividend yield of 1.3%; the five purchased 0.7%; and the five sold were yielding 2.6%. Why the shift? Performance!

What does this mean? A select group of big-cap stocks have become today's Nifty-Fifty. Moreover, the more money that is being invested into these same stocks, the greater the reason for more money to be invested into them! To say it another way, "the stocks are rising simply because they are rising!"

How important is it just to be a member of the S&P 500? Consider Progressive Corp., a large insurance company whose stock more than tripled in the prior thirty-one months. During a week in which the Dow advanced less than 1%, the share price of PGR jumped to 109 3/4 from 99 1/2 simply because it was added to the S&P 500 Index.

One of the glaring characteristics of the 1972 Nifty-Fifty Era was the similarity in stock patterns between the top-tier names of that so-called elite group, as illustrated in the earlier section. They all seemed to begin their moves up at the same time, they all peaked at almost the same time, and they all plunged with a stock-crash ferocity, hitting the bottom together in 1974. Remember our five quality-stock examples? As a group, they declined 76%, top to bottom! A concentration of this type is happening again today with the top-tier names: Merck, Coca Cola, Procter & Gamble, Exxon, General Electric, and so on.

Another reason to be concerned is a misinterpretation of "growth" with mutual funds. When a fund holder reviews the performance of his or her fund portfolio at the end of any quarter and Fund "X" has increased in value, say, 5% (perhaps matching the S&P 500) while Fund "Y" declined 2% in the same period, the investor might assume that Fund X is growing, while Fund Y is not. In reality, the annual growth of the companies held by Fund X might be only 7% for the next five years, while Fund Y companies could be expecting growth of 12%. If Fund Y is sold to buy more of the "faster-growing" Fund X, the investor could be contributing, unknowingly, to THE GREAT INDEX MANIA.

Again, recall our earlier discussion of the 1970-74 Nifty-Fifty Era. Between the high of 1972 and the bottom in late 1974, the Dow Jones Average declined almost 47% while many of the elite Nifty-Fifty stocks lost more than 70% of their market value. Today, much of the Nifty-Fifty *is* the Dow.

When these big-caps fall from grace, will the rest of the market remain undisturbed? Maybe, but it's doubtful, because these are the very same stocks that investors are watching when they ask: "How's the market today, Sam?"

Have the price advances of these "index-type" stocks been running wildly ahead of their fundamentals, as it happened in 1970-72? And if so, by how much? This key question will be discussed later in this book.

CHAPTER THREE
IT'S GONE "PARABOLIC!"

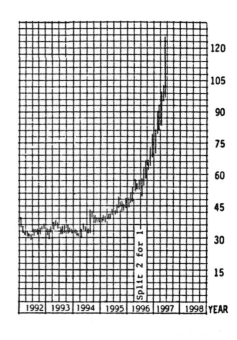

It's Gone "Parabolic!"

The chart pattern is unmistakable! The price begins its climb, gradually at first, then a bit more rapidly. Soon it appears to be advancing in an almost vertical direction! "How can this continue?" investors ask. Since the beginning of time, the answer is always the same: "It can't." Why?

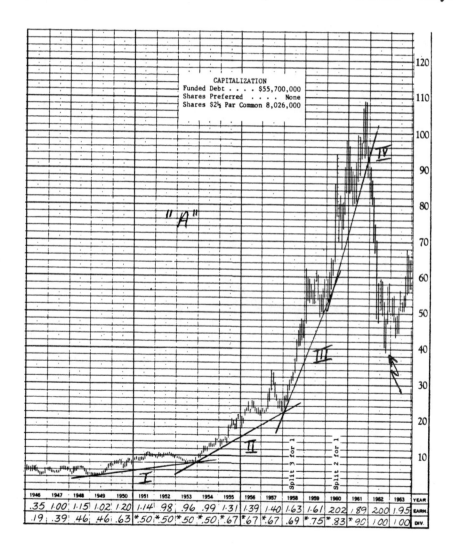

	1946	1947	1948	1949	1950	1951	1952	1953	1954	1955	1956	1957	1958	1959	1960	1961	1962	1963	YEAR
EARN.	.35	1.00	1.15	1.02	1.20	1.14	.98	.96	.99	1.31	1.39	1.40	1.63	1.61	2.02	1.89	2.00	1.95	
DIV.	.19	.39	.46	.46	.63	*.50	*.50	*.50	*.50	*.67	*.67	*.67	.69	*.75	*.83	*.90	1.00	1.00	

CAPITALIZATION
Funded Debt $55,700,000
Shares Preferred . . . . None
Shares $2½ Par Common 8,026,000

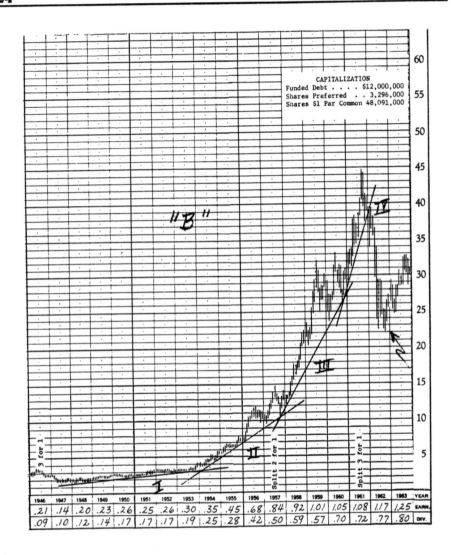

YEAR	1946	1947	1948	1949	1950	1951	1952	1953	1954	1955	1956	1957	1958	1959	1960	1961	1962	1963
EARN.	.21	.14	.20	.23	.26	.25	.26	.30	.35	.45	.68	.84	.92	1.01	1.05	1.08	1.17	1.25
DIV.	.09	.10	.12	.14	.17	.17	.17	.19	.25	.28	.42	.50	.59	.57	.70	.72	.77	.80

CAPITALIZATION
Funded Debt $12,000,000
Shares Preferred . . 3,296,000
Snares $1 Par Common 48,091,000

Because, whether it is a stock, an average of the market, or the price of sugar, the fundamentals are *never* able to keep up with a parabolic price advance.

There is one rule, however, that can be applied to all parabolic charts. If the fundamentals are improving rapidly, and not about to reverse, the decline that is certain to follow will be less severe.

Compare the two "generic" parabolic chart patterns illustrated here. The shares of both companies advanced smartly, but "went parabolic" in late 1957. The price of the first stock ("A") rose 395% to its 1961 peak and then declined 64% to its low in 1962. The second stock ("B") advanced 326%, and then dropped 51% in the same timeframe. At the lows of the 1974 bear market, twelve years later, what was the price of each stock?

The correct answer is, you cannot possibly tell from these two pictures. However, "A" was $3 per share, and "B" was $96 per share. Company "B" enjoyed excellent growth while "A" did not. The fact is, the financial condition and long term growth of each company will determine the long term performance of each stock.* And the same is true for the stock market.

Does this mean charts of this type are useless? No. Actually, they are worthy of review and comparison. Notice that the climb of each began in 1948 and continued in four stages: 1948 to 1953; 1953 to 1957; and 1957 to 1960, with the fourth and final stage occurring from that point to the peak. Notice, too, that each stock dropped to a level just below that (1960) point. True, "A" may have advanced more sharply, but it also encountered a more dramatic selloff than did "B." And, finally, note that "A" retraced *two-thirds* of its 1953-1961 advance; whereas, "B" retraced only *half*.

A comparison of the parabolic chart patterns of the 1921-1929 period and the 1974-1987 period reveals much the same story as "A" and "B" shown here. Also, note the monthly charts in Appendix A which illustrate many of today's index fund favorites.

---

* In real life, "A" was Addressograph-Multigraph Corp., and "B" was American Home Products.

1929

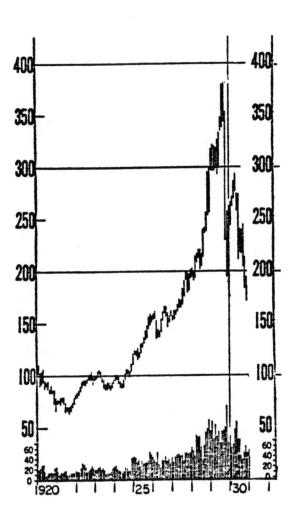

1987

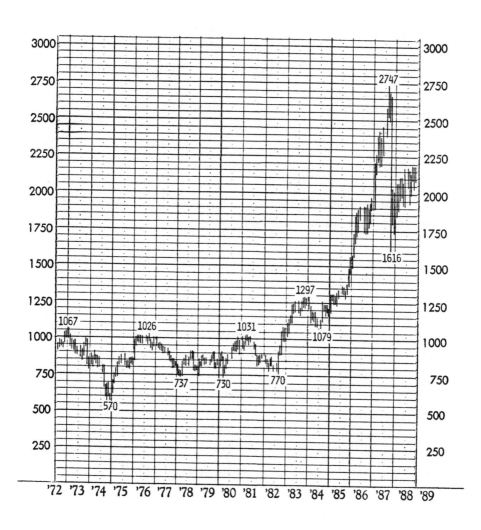

Finally, the next page presents another classic illustration of this "blowoff" pattern -- the price of gold when it went parabolic in 1979. Whether it is a stock or a commodity, the general rule for this pattern is simple. The price should crash to a point located between II and III and then recover 50% of the decline (note the arrows on the chart). Once this rally is complete, the fundamentals will dictate the future direction of prices.

Today, more than fifteen years later, it should be noted that gold has not yet declined below its key 1982/84 price levels. This is not considered a good omen for the U.S. economy if you are an investor concerned about inflation longer term. For this reason, the price of gold will be watched closely if it ever declines again below $300 per ounce. People worried about a repeat of the deflationary experience of the 1930's will be watching that price level for much the same reason.

As a fundamental example of the above, note from the earlier charts that stocks continued their decline in October, 1930, by falling through the 195.35 November low of 1929 thus ushering in "The Great Depression." In contrast to this, prices resumed the bull market when they rose above the crash point of two years earlier in 1989. Clearly, the fundamentals for these two periods were totally different.

The price of gold and its technical picture is being presented here because, over the next two or three years, the never-ending controversy between inflation and deflation is likely to be debated further. Gold is an important ingredient in that debate and understanding the technical outlook for gold prices should prove very helpful in that discussion.

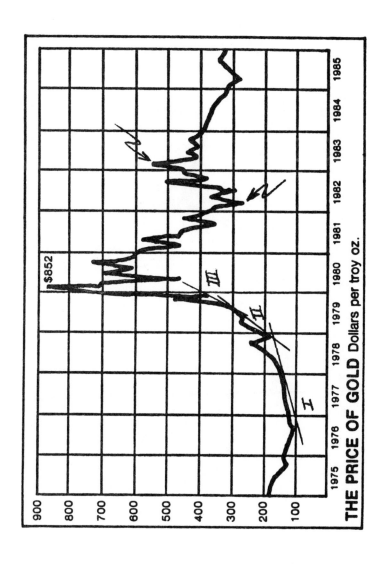

THE PRICE OF GOLD Dollars per troy oz.

CHAPTER FOUR
THE CRASH "PATTERN"

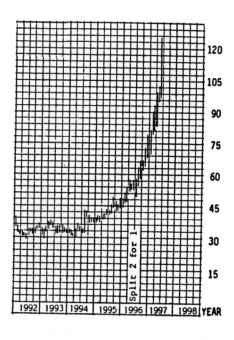

The Crash "Pattern"
The "A/G Method"

Although it is impossible to say whether the chart patterns of 1929 and 1987 will ever repeat in the same way again, the fact that they were so similar, and that variations can be found elsewhere, means that a discussion of stock crashes and bear markets would never be complete without this segment. The precision of the patterns of these two events which were fifty-eight years apart is nothing short of extraordinary, and eerie at the very least.

When studying the following comparisons, keep these few thoughts in mind. First, in both instances, the market tops were formed in exactly twenty-one weeks and both "crashed" in two emotional, record-volume sessions wiping out half of all gains enjoyed in the prior twenty-two months. In 1929, the crash hit bottom 45% below the peak of eight weeks earlier; whereas in 1987, it was 41% over the same timeframe.

Second, the two events were not comparable fundamentally. The economies and the circumstances were different, and as a result, the market trends following the technical recoveries of both crashes were totally opposite. In other words, these charts are essentially pictures of raw emotion in action.

Ordinarily, these two stock market patterns would be dismissed as a mere coincidence. However, this chapter illustrates two other contemporary examples when variations of this pattern were seen in a less-stressful environment. In the first case (1966), the decline amounted to 27%, top to bottom. In the second example (1968-70), it was 37%. So the lesson is clear. Don't underestimate the possibility of history repeating when it comes to the stock market.

The first chart shows the final phases of the 1929 top, extending from the Spring of 1929 into November, just after the crash. On the chart (weekly closing DJIA prices), note the specific points labeled "a" through "g".

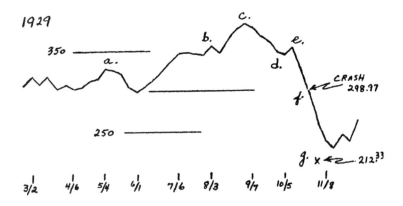

The next chart below illustrates exactly the same monthly timeframe for the Dow fifty-eight years later. Once again, note the points labeled "a" through "g".

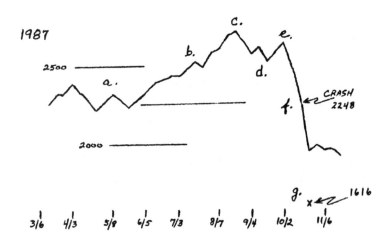

When comparing the two charts, notice that each crash occurred from roughly the same level (the weekly closings of 297 in 1929 and 2240 in 1987, located at the trough between "a" and "b"). These early-summer points also occurred exactly 21 weeks prior to the actual crash in each case. Moreover, the peaks (labeled "c") of 386 in 1929 and 2747 in 1987 preceded each crash by exactly eight weeks. Also, both crash points ("f") marked the halfway points, top to bottom.

Contrary to the history books, the 1929 stock market crash was actually a two-day event (October 28 and October 29) following the 298.97 weekly close on October 26. The 1987 crash was also a two-day event. The Dow Jones Industrial Average closed at 2248 on Friday, the 16th of October, dropped a whopping 508 points on Monday, October 19th, then dropped further before reversing on Tuesday, just as it did in 1929.

Finally, it is worth noting that the intraday lows of both stock market crashes retraced essentially all of the gains enjoyed within the prior two years (ie., 1928/29 and 1986/87). In 1928, the Dow started the year at about 200; while the new year 1986 began just above 1500.

The A/G Method was discovered by the author more than thirty years ago, but was never applied in any serious way until the 1987 market was later compared to 1929. The conclusion of that study appears in this book.

For readers who find these observations of interest, there have been many pioneers in the area of pattern recognition and their writings are recommended. They include Ralph Nelson Elliott and two students of his work, A.J. Frost and Robert Prechter, Jr., as well as the late Edson Gould. Also worth reading is the book, *Technical Analysis of Stock Trends*, by Robert Edwards and John Magee.

The A/G pattern is, perhaps, most closely related to another that has been widely used for decades, the "Head & Shoulders" formation, which is explained further in "The Principles of Technical Analysis" chapter in *Understanding Wall Street*. Below is a weekly chart of the market top in 1961-62. It displays a classic head & shoulders pattern. Next, look back to see how "b", "c" and "e" formed the head and shoulders during 1929 and 1987.

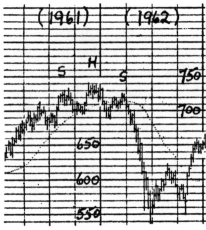

Those who apply the A/G Method over time will discover a few variations from the basic pattern illustrated here. All told, many of the most serious market declines in the past seventy years have developed from this particular formation.

It happens something like this: Point "a" represents the start of the pattern. However, usually, points "a" and "b" are not identified until point "c" is suspected. Point "b" is always well above "a," and the trough between "a" and "b" is important because it later becomes the "crash point." Point "c" is always above "b" and typically 5 to 15 weeks later. Point "d" is the trough between "c" and the "last-gasp rally" ending with "e." Point "f" is the "crash point" and it is normally the halfway point between the top ("c") and the final low.

Below is the 1966 market, first, as most technicians view it, with the "head & shoulders" formation noted. The specific A/G points were added to the other chart. Compare the 1965-66 top to the 1929 and 1987 charts. Notice how the "crash point" held initially after a drop of 140 points (1000-860). Once the market resumed its descent, "crashing" below 860, the target became 720 (860-140). A 720 target wasn't too far off, considering the actual DJIA low was eventually 736.

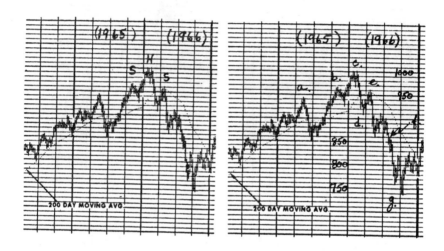

In both 1929 and 1987, the market didn't hesitate, opening with "gaps" down on the opening trades of the new week. In both instances, traders were given a reason to sleep poorly on Sunday night. This sudden panic activity when trading begins the next session is what we now call a "crash." When it occurs, it almost always happens with a "gap-down-opening" the next trading day, and it frequently starts a new week off with a "bang."

The next set of charts illustrates a similar story for the top of the 1968-70 bear market. The final low occurred in mid-1970 at 627. This formation is a particularly interesting variation because the downside target, originally calculated to be 735 (ie., 995, labeled "c," less 865, labeled "2"), later became 635 (995, less 815, labeled "1"). This possibility was signaled as such because the left shoulder was represented by "a" rather than "b." Again, the actual DJIA low came reasonably close to the target.

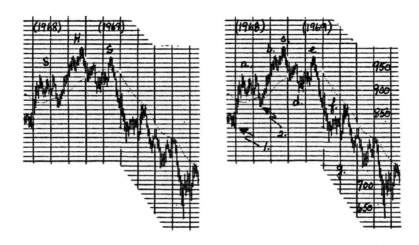

Returning to the 1929 chart, this is how the target for that crash was calculated... The intraday low between "a" and "b" was 290.02 set on May 31. The high (intraday) was 386.10, hit on September 3. The target was, therefore, 193.94. The crash low was 212.33, but the lowest price recorded before the 1930 recovery rally was 195.35, set on November 13, 1929.

The 1987 target was calculated in exactly the same manner... The intraday low between "a" and "b" was 2188 set on May 20. On August 25, the intraday peak ("c") was established at 2747. So, the target became 1629. The intraday low on October 20 was 1616, and that was also the lowest figure recorded after the crash.

Remain Alert and Be Patient

A multi-year parabolic market is an exciting event to behold with gains of 100%, 300%, or even 1000% not uncommon. Serious students of finance like to compare it to a comets. Markets of this type are witnessed only once or twice in a lifetime. While they may occur infrequently, when they do, the ascent can be most rewarding if the right stocks are in the portfolio, and the descent can be nothing less than breathtaking for almost every serious investor.

As we look back into history, there are two important lessons to remember regarding stock market crashes:

First, the most devastating portion typically occurs during the second half of the decline, and that happens quickly and unexpectedly for most participants. By that time, it is often too late to take any action. The damage has been done.

Second, a major stock market top normally takes time to develop. In 1929, being the most classic example, stocks traded within 12% of the exact high for at least 14-15 weeks. The same was true in 1937 when stocks shed 50% of their value, with most of it lost in a short eight-week period. A great many issues failed to recover for more than seven years.

Judging by the way the current bull market has developed both fundamentally and technically, the next bear market promises to be substantial. The stock market has, indeed, been rising simply because it has been rising. Still, an alert investor should have enough time to react as the warnings and events leading to the crash unfold. As this book suggests, the last and most dramatic stage of this multi-year event already appears to be in motion.

CHAPTER FIVE
PREDICTING SHORT TERM MOVES

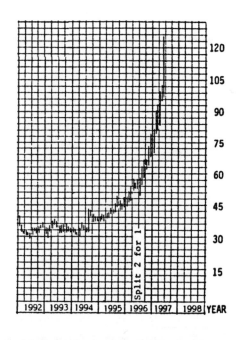

Predicting Short Term Moves

The daily activities on most worldwide exchanges today are heavily influenced by computer-oriented short term speculators, program traders, options and futures players, and arbitrageurs, to name just a few. Most of these people are only concerned with hourly or daily price movements. Try to imagine the activities of these players as ripples in an ocean, perhaps noticeable on each wave, but minor contributors to the tide you are trying to predict. The waves are, by far, much more useful as indicators.

For this reason, a unique software program, entitled The WALL STREET TRADER, was devised by the author in 1996. The program was created to provide traders and investors with a reliable method of identifying the intermediate moves (or "waves") to each bull or bear market. Entering data from the newspaper into the program requires about four minutes each day. A typical printout from The WALL STREET TRADER is presented on the next few pages (reduced in size, of course).

Included in this new program are four specific indicators and a "composite" (the Master Indicator, explained later):

Basic Indicator - A combination of option indicators, a Sentiment Indicator of newsletter writers, and the Specialist Short Sale Ratio.

Put/Call Ratios - Two individual (put/call) ratios of Index Options, each calculated with its own formula.

The Screw Factor - A measure of the relationship between option prices and volume over several days.

MASTER INDICATOR - A composite of most of the technical factors listed above. A BUY or SELL signal must be "confirmed" by at least three of the components.

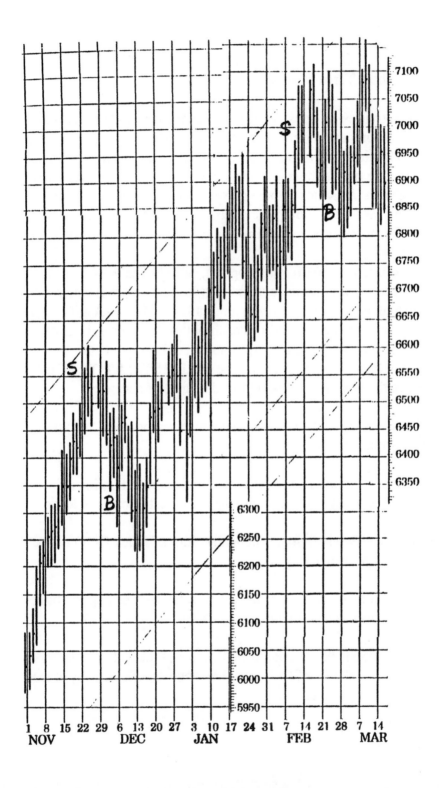

The WALL STREET TRADER

Date 1997	DJIA Close	Basic B 10.00- S 13.00+	Put / Call Ratios B 1.00- S 1.70+	B 50%- S 100%+	Screw Factor B 15%- S 25%+	MASTER INDICATOR B 100%- S 250%+	BUY/SELL (+3 Cnf)
Mar 10	7079	12.04	1.73	139.2%	24.9%	224%	neg.
Mar 4	6853	8.71	0.88	34.4%	18.8%	94%	Buy
Feb 28	6878	7.67 !	0.58	51.0%	11.1% !	73%	Buy
Feb 18	7067	13.24	1.47	123.9%	26.2%	293%	Sell
Feb 13	7022	14.52	2.51	149.5%	31.6%	401%	Sell !
Feb 12	6962	12.97	2.26	105.6%	31.1%	393%	Sell
Dec 31	6448	7.61 !	0.62	4.0% !	12.2%	49%	Buy !
Dec 26	6547	12.69	2.13	113.8%	30.6%	302%	Sell
Dec 12	6304	8.21	0.90	35.5%	12.7%	45%	Buy !
Dec 3	6443	10.00	0.97	7.5% !	14.0%	49%	Buy
Nov 25	6547	13.59	2.20	105.4%	21.2%	452%	Sell

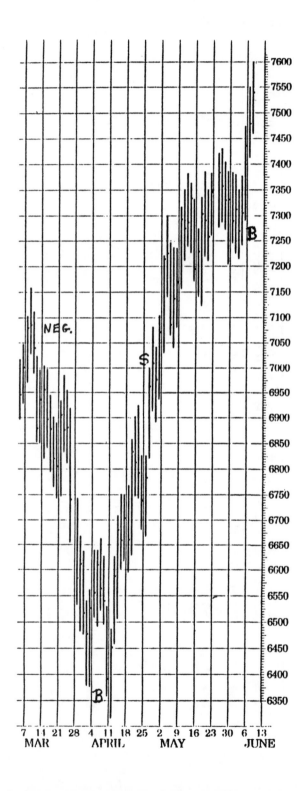

The WALL STREET TRADER

Date 1997	DJIA Close	Basic B 10.00- S 13.00+	Put / Call Ratios B 1.00- S 1.70+	B 50%- S 100%+	Screw Factor B 15%- S 25%+	MASTER INDICATOR B 100%- S 250%+	BUY/SELL (+3 Cnf)
May 15	7334	12.82	0.87	83.8%	24.7%	225%	
May 7	7086	10.57	0.68	39.1%	17.7%	158%	
May 5	7214	16.20 !	3.44	233.3% !	41.9% !	727%	Sell!
May 2	7071	14.29	2.04	171.8% !	31.9%	498%	Sell!
Apr 30	7009	13.57	2.54	76.3%	25.7%	314%	Sell
Apr 29	6962	13.10	2.29	183.6% !	32.8%	459%	Sell!
Apr 11	6392	7.25 !	0.87	37.5%	8.2% !	72%	Buy !
Apr 8	6609	13.18	1.78	84.2%	32.6%	276%	Sell
Apr 7	6556	13.17	2.18	81.4%	28.0%	262%	Sell
Apr 4	6526	12.79	2.17	122.8%	33.5%	316%	Sell
Apr 1	6611	8.43	0.85	22.4%	13.0%	85%	Buy !
Mar 31	6583	8.69	0.90	53.9%	12.3%	84%	Buy

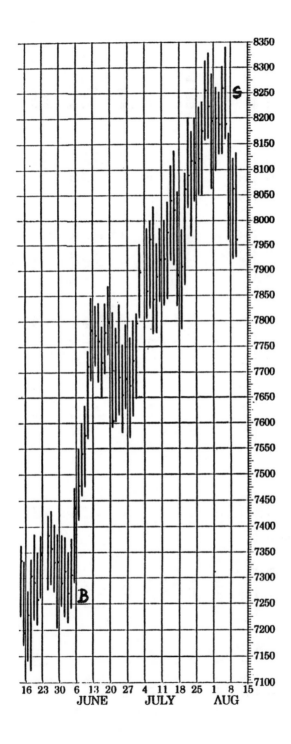

The WALL STREET TRADER

Date 1997	DJIA Close	Basic B 10.00- S 13.00+	Put / Call Ratios B 1.00- S 1.70+	B 50%- S 100%+	Screw Factor B 15%- S 25%+	MASTER INDICATOR B 100%- S 250%+	BUY/SELL (+3 Cnf)
Aug 6	8259	13.41	1.91	117.7%	22.7%	337%	Sell
Aug 5	8188	13.81	1.38	102.5%	25.9%	342%	Sell
Jul 21	7906	8.97	0.69	29.9%	12.5%	66%	Buy !
Jul 18	7890	9.57	0.98	23.9%	14.1%	91%	Buy !
Jul 9	7842	8.68	0.89	13.6% !	10.5% !	92%	Buy !
Jul 3	7896	14.53	1.94	100.7%	24.4%	288%	Sell
Jul 2	7795	14.41	1.75	125.9%	39.2%	454%	Sell!
Jun 23	7604	8.69	0.91	29.3%	6.3% !	29%	Buy !
Jun 19	7777	13.92	1.59	172.4%	27.9%	284%	Sell
Jun 17	7761	14.73	1.83	124.3%	39.8%	293%	Sell!
Jun 16	7772	13.67	1.76	90.3%	27.7%	272%	Sell
Jun 4	7270	9.40	1.03	35.5%	10.7% !	66%	Buy

The WALL STREET TRADER features a "Master Indicator" that serves as the primary guide. Whenever it registers a BUY or a SELL signal, it must be accompanied (or, as technicians like to say, "confirmed") with a corresponding signal by at least three of the other four. A reading below 100% registers a "Buy," and above 250% is "Sell." To repeat, these readings, while quite accurate as the record shows, are primarily short term in nature and should be used by long term investors as an "early warning signal," or a reason to question the direction of the market near term, but nothing more. Otherwise, it is, as its title suggests, primarily a trader's tool. (See Appendix C and/or write or call the publisher for additional details).

The "Principles of Technical Analysis" chapter of *Understanding Wall Street* explains a few other technical indicators designed to help investors anticipate reversals in price trends. There are many proven methods from which to chose. Among them are the "Member Short Sales Ratio" and the "Specialist Short Sales Ratio." Both are explained in the book and the figures needed for their calculations can be found each week in the "Market Laboratory" section of *Barron's*.

Many market observers monitor the "market breadth" of the New York Stock Exchange and NASDAQ (ie., cumulative totals of the daily advances & declines, as well as the highs & lows recorded each day). Some believe these figures can help spot market trouble sooner than otherwise.

Also, many technicians employ the use of "moving averages" to judge the direction of the overall market. Most popular is the 200-day moving average coupled with a shorter term average such as a 10-week moving average. The concept here is simple ..."the trend is your friend," or "it's okay to miss the top or bottom as long as you are in during most of the rise and out during most of the decline." However, when it comes to stock market crashes, moving averages are generally useless because the move is rapid. By the time action needs to be taken it's too late.

To repeat, it is important for the long term investor to see the "big picture" and not be unduly influenced by the "noise" created in the form of very short term market swings. This generally means long term investors today should not be overly concerned with moves of less than 5%-8% (or about 400-600 DJIA points).

Finally, there are hundreds of newsletters written by experienced and respected analysts such as Arch Crawford, Marty Zweig, and others. Many of these writers maintain their own indicators and have superior records calling the short term swings of the market. However, this is a matter of personal choice and, as such, specific newsletters will not be endorsed here.

CHAPTER SIX
A LONG TERM PERSPECTIVE

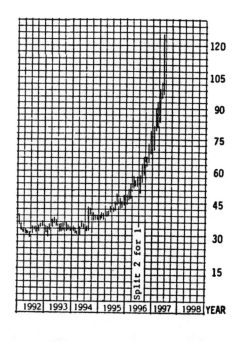

A Long Term Perspective

Johnson & Johnson

Thirty-five years is a long time. For many investing in the stock market today it represents an almost-unrealistic timeframe to consider. Still, as the Johnson & Johnson charts in this chapter show, few companies have attained a growth record more rewarding than this one. A study of this premier investment as it grew might offer a few valuable lessons for today's equity investors and market observers.

When the Johnson brothers incorporated their new business as Johnson & Johnson in 1887, they might have never imagined that their New Brunswick, New Jersey enterprise would, seventy-five years later (1962), be a thriving company reporting earnings of $18 million on sales exceeding $350 million.

Any investor so unlucky to have bought JNJ stock at the highest price in 1962 had to be willing to pay 37.2 times the earnings per share reported for that year. And, sadly, within six months of that purchase, additional shares could have been acquired at a price at least 40% lower. However, the stock appeared to be well on the road to recovery throughout most of 1963. All the while, the company's prospects appeared as bright as ever. Johnson & Johnson's 1963 profits were later reported to be 13% above the 1962 figure and a 20%+ gain seemed possible for 1964, well above our investor's estimate of 17-18% annual growth longer term.

JOHNSON & JOHNSON

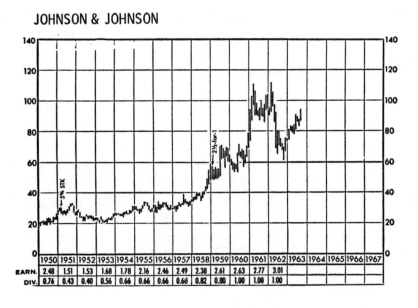

In early 1965, the price of Johnson & Johnson finally moved comfortably above the high established three years earlier. Assuming our 1962 investor had the confidence and patience to hold, or even buy more throughout this period, the investment was now, finally, beginning to bear fruit.

Seven years later, by mid-1972, Johnson & Johnson had risen to a quote roughly ten times the original purchase price, by virtue of a 20.7% average annual eps growth rate and a 1972 price/earnings multiple of 61.4! Between 1962 and 1972, the stock had risen in a parabolic manner, splitting 3 for 1 in 1967 and 3 for 1 again in 1970. In only one year between 1963 and 1972 did JNJ report an annual earnings growth rate below 17.5% (13.4% in 1967) and in four of those years, the growth rate exceeded 20% (1964, 1965, 1968, and 1971). JNJ had become one of the famed "Nifty-Fifty" stocks. It was a "10-bagger," as Peter Lynch, a noted money manager, was fond of saying.

By 1970, Johnson & Johnson had joined the "Billion Dollar Club" and now, in 1972, sales were nearly four times the revenue figure reported ten years earlier. And, to the delight of our 1962 investor, the dividend checks arriving from the company each year were now totalling about 4.3% of the original "hapless" investment. So, with the prospects of a somewhat slower (14-16%) long term growth rate, what does an investor do with a 61 P/E?

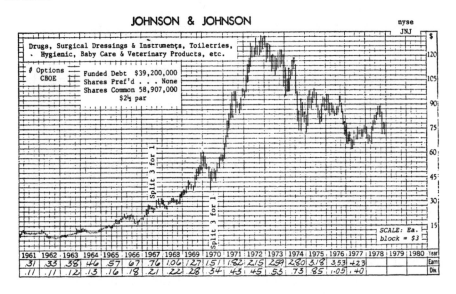

This is the continuous and never-ending story of investing in good, long term growth stocks. Any investor so unlucky to have bought Johnson & Johnson stock at the highest price in 1972 had to be willing to pay 61.4 times the earnings per share reported for that year. And, sadly, within two years, additional shares could have been acquired at a price at least 45% lower. Even though Johnson & Johnson's profits between 1973 and 1982 grew steadily at a 14.6% annual rate, the stock underperformed badly and did not return to its 1972 peak price until ten years later. Does this all sound familiar??

By mid-1997, Johnson & Johnson was sporting a P/E ratio of 26.6 times the expected $2.50 per share for the year. If analysts' estimates of a 13-16% long term growth rate prove correct, then the stock, relative to its expected growth rate, would not be much more overvalued than it was at its highs in 1962, 1972, or in 1987 when the stock peaked at 21 times earnings, or 1.3 times its growth rate.

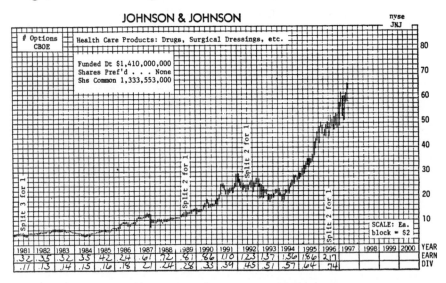

So, how does a company with $22-24 billion in sales manage to grow 13-16% per year over the next several years? If there is any company that can, JNJ would be it. Like 3M and a few other premier companies, JNJ is comprised of many subsidiaries that are run independently. Still, Johnson & Johnson is facing the same dilemma most other big-cap blue chips are facing. How can ANY company grow earnings fast enough to justify its stock price when profit margins are already at historically-high levels and *the stock is rising simply because it is rising*? The answer is, "it probably can't." And, due to its size, even a 10% rate might be a challenge within a few years.

Based on this JNJ study, it can be concluded that whenever the stock's price/earnings multiple exceeded its growth rate by a factor of TWO, years of underperformance usually follow. It is also apparent that JNJ finds market support once it returns to a P/E multiple closer to its expected rate of eps growth.

And what has been learned from this study?

First, all investors should make an effort to know the company, understand its prospects and true underlying growth rate, and learn to recognize when a stock is fully-valued and when it's not.

Second, with patience, over an extended period of time, building a position in the right stock through dollar-cost-averaging can create substantial wealth. At the lowest price after the 1972-74 debacle, JNJ stock was still FIVE TIMES its highest price in 1962. And at its lowest price after the 1987 crash, it was still 25% above its grossly-overvalued quotes of 1972.

Third, even great investments like this can punish investors with years of underperformance if the stock is bought, ignoring common sense, and with a complete disregard for valuation.

And, finally, since most of these great companies tend to rise and fall together affecting entire portfolios in a dramatic manner, the shorter the investment horizon, the greater the need for attention to valuation and investment timing.

Johnson & Johnson happens to be one of the elite members of the Dow Jones Industrial Average. Is JNJ an exception or an example as we study the other index fund favorites?

General Electric

If ever there was a "proxy" for the Dow Jones Industrial Average since the mid-1950's, or maybe earlier, General Electric would be it! Just as the Dow Average has a more contemporary look today with a few new names, so does GE. In years past, this conglomerate had a far greater dependence on industrial supplies and equipment. Today, about 37% of revenues is derived from its financial arm, GE Capital, and the success this company has enjoyed in its "white-collar" businesses, such as finance and broadcasting, has helped reward shareholders with a growth in net income of almost 12% annually for more than two decades.

Under the able leadership of Jack F. Welch, chairman and CEO, the company has been concentrating its expansion into the service segment of the economy. For example, for many years, General Electric has been a leading producer of aircraft engines. Yet, GE's expansion in this area has been focused more recently on the servicing and maintenance of them.

Revenues are now approaching $100 billion and the total market value at this writing is greater than any other company in the world. And, like most of the other leading companies in recent years, GE has cut costs internally and repurchased shares in the open market. Although the company remains highly cyclical, whenever the economic environment is positive, as it has been recently, GE's results reflect it.

When projecting GE's growth into the future, size becomes an obstacle to some degree. For General Electric to increase its revenues 10% per year, it must, for example, grow the equivalent of a Colgate-Palmolive Company or a Monsanto Company EVERY TWELVE MONTHS.

GENERAL ELECTRIC COMPANY

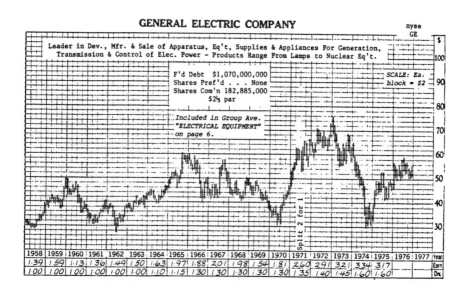

nyse
GE

Leader in Dev., Mfr. & Sale of Apparatus, Eq't, Supplies & Appliances For Generation, Transmission & Control of Elec. Power - Products Range From Lamps to Nuclear Eq't.

F'd Debt $1,070,000,000
Shares Pref'd . . . None
Shares Com'n 182,885,000
$2½ par

SCALE: Ea.
block = $2

Included in Group Ave.
"ELECTRICAL EQUIPMENT"
on page 6.

Split 2 for 1

Year	1958	1959	1960	1961	1962	1963	1964	1965	1966	1967	1968	1969	1970	1971	1972	1973	1974	1975	1976	1977
Earn	1.39	1.59	1.13	1.36	1.49	1.50	1.63	1.97	1.88	2.01	1.98	1.54	1.81	2.60	2.91	3.21	3.34	3.17		
Div.	1.00	1.00	1.00	1.00	1.00	1.00	1.10	1.15	1.30	1.30	1.30	1.30	1.30	1.35	1.40	1.45	1.60	1.60		

GENERAL ELECTRIC COMPANY

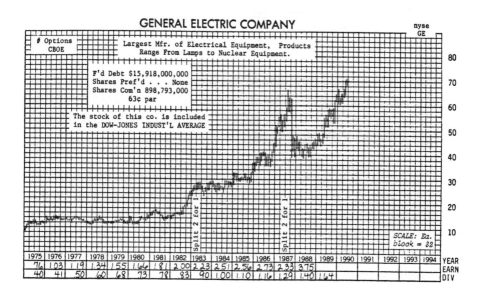

nyse
GE

Options
CBOE

Largest Mfr. of Electrical Equipment, Products Range From Lamps to Nuclear Equipment.

F'd Debt $15,918,000,000
Shares Pref'd . . . None
Shares Com'n 898,793,000
63¢ par

The stock of this co. is included in the DOW-JONES INDUST'L AVERAGE

Split 2 for 1

Split 2 for 1

SCALE: Ea.
block = $2

YEAR	1975	1976	1977	1978	1979	1980	1981	1982	1983	1984	1985	1986	1987	1988	1989	1990	1991	1992	1993	1994
EARN	76	1.03	1.19	1.34	1.55	1.66	1.81	2.00	2.23	2.51	2.56	2.73	2.33	3.75						
DIV	40	41	50	60	68	73	78	83	90	1.00	1.10	1.16	1.29	1.40	1.64					

Assuming GE's underlying growth rate is 11-12% over the next year or two, but only 8-9% over an extended period of time, a price/earnings ratio approaching 30 times, as it is currently, appears very generous, even considering the changed nature of its businesses.

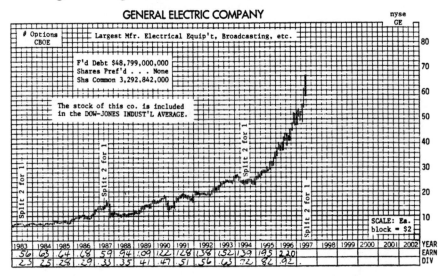

The monthly charts used throughout this book are from M.C. Horsey & Company, Inc., publishers of *The Stock Picture*.* They are favored for this particular text because they do, indeed, provide investors with a longer term perspective on individual issues.

Compare, for example, the GE charts shown on the previous page as well as the one above. On many popular charts, stock split adjustments tend to mask the longer term perspective, especially when only a few years of stock prices are available. The extraordinary gains big-cap investors have enjoyed over the past few years, not to mention the risks inherent today, are especially evident with these charts.

* M.C. Horsey & Co., (410) 742-3700

CHAPTER SEVEN
THE FUNDAMENTALS: PAST & PRESENT

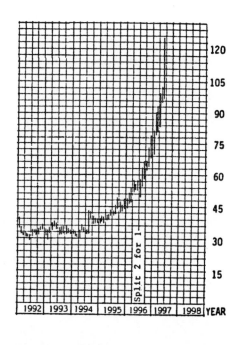

The Fundamentals: Past & Present

At one time or another, every analyst on Wall Street has heard this cynical comment, "Don't tell me what to buy, or when, just tell me when to SELL."

This is no easy task, to be sure, especially when the stock market has, as they say, "gone parabolic." What's the difference between an 18 P/E, or a 25 P/E, or a 40 P/E? Once prices have gone so high, beyond the point of discounting any earnings and dividend potential for years to come, the adjustment to follow is certain to be severe as it returns to earth.

So, therefore, "What is 'earth'?" How bad could it be if most companies enter a period of slower growth, as they did in the late 60's, or if the investment mood changes, as it did in the early 70's? Or, worse yet, how low could prices go assuming a combination of both ills? Is it possible to determine some degree of vulnerability as we did with JNJ?

In 1946, the first post-WWII year, earnings "per share" of the Dow Jones Industrial Average was 13.63. In 1996, the reported figure was 353.88, and it could exceed 400 in 1997 for the first time in history. Thus, for the past fifty years, earnings for the DJIA increased at an average annual rate of about 6.7%.

Assuming the U.S. will continue to enjoy its "new era" of peace and prosperity, and taking into account the recent replacements of faster-growing components into the Average, a higher growth rate of, say, 7%, does not appear unrealistic for the future. Observers should not overlook the fact that these companies are very large enterprises and, more importantly, we are probably now in the later stages of an economic cycle (assuming "cycles" still exist). Therefore, it would NOT be realistic to expect the growth rate of DJIA earnings to exceed 7% over the next few decades, including more good times, as we have seen recently, and some difficult periods as well.

Estimating growth for the DJIA on a company-by-company basis also suggests an underlying growth rate of about 7%. Obviously, a company like Johnson & Johnson has a good chance of attaining a 9% growth rate which would be needed to offset slower-growing companies like GM, Union Carbide, and Chevron. It should also be remembered that a 7% growth rate is an acceptable number within the context of a national economy growing at a rate below 4%, as it has in recent years.

Also, during the 1946-96 period there was a tendency for the P/E of the DJIA to range between 1.8 times and 2.2 times its growth rate (ie., a P/E of 12 to 15 times earnings) while the average P/E was about 13.5, or twice the growth rate. There have been only a few times over the past fifty years when the P/E of the DJIA rose to more than three times its long term growth rate. Now is one of those times.

A table appears in *Understanding Wall Street*, Third Edition, page 114, that suggests a series of adequate price earnings ratios, considering two important variables: the GROWTH RATE and the level of INTEREST RATES (Aaa bonds). The original idea was advanced by the late Benjamin Graham, co-author of a classic book entitled *Security Analysis*. According to the table, a 7% expected growth rate could command the following P/E ratios at these interest rates: 6% (16.5x); 7% (14.2x); 8% (12.4x). Assuming the long term trend of interest rates will continue down somewhat in the years ahead, a price/earnings ratio in the middle of this range seems most appropriate.

Over the past twenty or thirty years investors have learned to recognize the inverse relationship between P/E ratios and interest rates (notice the figures in the prior paragraph). So, for this reason, one must also focus on the environment as well as earnings growth. In fact, they are very much related.

Today's Investment Scene

In recent years, the word "productivity" has taken a new meaning on Wall Street giving investors, analysts, and portfolio managers a "warm and fuzzy" feeling. Whenever a company announces its intention to "restructure" (an attempt to reverse past mistakes), and "downsize" (that is, to close less-profitable facilities and fire workers), and to "repurchase shares" (use the company's cash to buy its fully-priced shares in the open market), the stock usually rises on the news. Many employees who were fired, might cringe at the memorable scene in the movie "Wall Street." In it, money manager Gordon Gecko addressed a shareholders' meeting with a bold statement: "Greed is Good!"

To date, restructuring has been an extremely effective strategy for most companies. Over the past several decades a great many businesses had accumulated layers of redundancy at many levels. Now, this new attention to detail has, indeed, made companies, as some like to say, "lean and mean" and far more competitive in the fast-moving global marketplace.

The increase in productivity in recent years is REAL. Companies are now using personal computers in management and in operations, bar codes have helped control inventory and prices, and the internet and cellular phones have changed communications. For most companies, this has led to improved profit margins, greater returns on equity, and quarterly earnings reports that have surpassed almost every optimistic estimate. However, in many cases, sales growth has not been impressive and projecting any continuation of these profitability gains requires acquisitions (buying other companies that can be streamlined or restructured in a similar manner). Unfortunately, analysts and investors today are assuming that recent trends will continue on forever.

There is a big question now facing Corporate America: "Are you investing into new products and services to grow your company in the future? Or are you merely offering more of what the consumer already has in a more profitable way?" Historically, the country has thrived on new-product investment. Instead, it appears that companies today are applying their investment capital to speculate in the stock market.

Buybacks, as they are often called, are announced almost daily. In 1996, and again in 1997, buyback announcements have been running at almost twice the $95 billion announced in 1995 and up even more substantially from the $75-80 billion of 1994.

For those concerned about value, this is not a particularly healthy trend considering that stock prices today are roughly double what they were in 1994.

Given the inflation trends in recent years (see Appendix B), it should be no surprise that governments and the bureaucrats see little reason to go against the tide. Over the past year, Central Banks have been selling their inventories of GOLD, and this includes the gold-producing nation, Australia. Moreover, PETROLEUM stockpiles, built up as an insurance against another 1974 "oil crisis," are being reduced. It appears that the United States and Germany are fully confident that oil supplies will never again be interrupted and that oil-producing nations will remain entirely cooperative from now on – not a good assumption.

It is also no surprise that investors are enthusiastic about the meaningful opportunities for growth overseas. Indeed, the "globalization" of capitalism and the lower barriers for trade are encouraging. This is far different from the protectionist policies of, say, the 1920's. However, most larger companies are already enjoying substantial revenues from overseas, foreign competition is still intense, and the changing relationships of the currencies add a degree of uncertainty to the numbers.

Today, many observers use world trade as a rationalization for the excessive big-cap multiples. While overseas growth should definitely be included in any growth-rate calculations, there is certainly no reason to raise expectations for price/earnings relationships beyond what we've seen historically.

An Unsettling Comparison

Comparing the fundamentals of one period to another is usually a futile academic exercise. The economic circumstances and market forces are always very different. Nevertheless, a comparison of today's economic environment to that of the late 1920's is, in fact, quite interesting, to say the least.

First and foremost, there are several major differences between the 1926-1933 period and today. Important reforms put in place since then should not be dismissed because they are, for the most part, the result of many bad experiences from that earlier time. And, together, these factors are the primary reason why most market historians and economic experts dismiss any possibility that the United States will ever again see an economic depression of such magnitude.

The banking crises between October, 1930 and March, 1933 led to financial reforms including deposit insurance and a more flexible exchange system for international trade. The extremely high unemployment that occurred during the depression years led to the so-called "safety nets" for workers, including unemployment insurance. In the late 1920's, stocks could be bought with only 10% down. The rampant speculation that occurred at that time has since led to more-conservative (ie., 50%) margin rules in recent years. Also, since then, trading rules have changed placing many limits on the way stock prices can fluctuate during the day.

The change from an agricultural/industrial workforce to one that is far more service-oriented is an important distinction between the two periods. In addition, the protectionist and high-tariff policies of seventy years ago have been replaced with a much more open, free-trade government attitude today. Communications are now faster, global markets for products and services are much more extensive, and technology plays an important role today in virtually all aspects of finance and business.

However, the respective economic and investment environments between 1929 and today reveal an interesting and unsettling similarity. Whether these similarities or differences are good or bad could be subject to an optimistic or pessimistic interpretation ...

Inflation/Deflation: Between 1919 and 1921 the U.S. experienced a business recession and a sharp drop in wholesale prices (now referred to as producer prices). Until 1926, prices remained steady and then declined gradually throughout the remainder of the decade. After the stock market crash and beginning in 1930, however, wholesale prices renewed their sharp decline until the deflationary period came to an end three years later.

In some respects, the inflationary environment of recent years resembles the period of seventy years earlier. Economists have been referring to the steady decline in the rate of inflation since the 1990 recession as "disinflation." Most experts today agree that any snapshot of prices in this service economy is better represented by CPI (see Appendix B) than PPI.

Interest Rates and the Federal Reserve: In the late 1920's and until 1928, Federal Reserve policy was greatly influenced by the New York Bank, and its governor from inception, Benjamin Strong.

The death of Governor Strong in October, 1928 left the Federal Reserve without its most capable leader. Some experts have even speculated that had Benjamin Strong been alive and head of the New York Bank in the fall of 1930, he would have very likely recognized the liquidity crisis and taken more aggressive measures to head off the crises that followed.

Measured by the Discount Rate, Federal Reserve policies favored easy money in the late 1920's. In 1926, and again in 1927, the Discount Rate ranged between 3.5% and 4.0%. In 1928, it ranged between 3.5% and

5.0% and remained at 5.0% through 1929, until August, when it was increased to 6.0% reflecting strong growth reported for the months preceding. However, in retrospect, the Federal Reserve was clearly not "ahead of the curve" in 1929. The Fed reduced the rate back to 5.0% immediately following the stock market crash and then dropped it again to 4.5% before year end. The year 1930 saw a series of continuing declines to 2.5% by June, and to 2.0% just as the new year 1931 commenced.

The onset of the 1990 recession marked the peak in the Discount Rate at 7.0% Beginning that year, the Federal Reserve reduced it in a series of steps that ended at 3.0% in mid-1992 where it remained throughout 1993 and into early 1994. In 1994, the Fed increased the Discount Rate four times to 5.25% where it remained through 1995. Wall Street celebrated when Fed Chariman Alan Greenspan reduced the rate back to 5.0% as 1995 came to a close, and the Discount Rate is at that same level at this writing.

The yields on U.S. Government bonds were just under 4% and stocks (with higher payout ratios than today) were paying close to 3% in 1929. Now, the Government's 30-year bond is close to 6.5% and stock yields are less than 2%.

It is fair to say that the trends and levels of interest rates in recent years are not too dissimilar to late in that decade seventy years ago.

Industrial Production: In August, 1929, industrial production in the United States peaked at roughly 20% above their levels at the start of 1928 and about 50% above the levels of five years earlier, in mid-1924. The steady spurt of business activity that began in early 1928 extended a full nineteen months. And the "new era" was being celebrated with record high stock prices and glowing earnings reports and increased dividends from companies sharing in the prosperity.

By August, 1997, industrial production reached a level about 27% above the recession low point of early 1991. The steady climb in industrial activity over these past several years has been accompanied by higher productivity, as discussed earlier, glowing earnings reports, and increased dividends. It can be said that the U.S. has enjoyed steady growth in recent years but to a more modest degree than the less-mature economy of the 1920's.

Unemployment Rate: The jobless rate declined from well above 6% in the recession year 1921 to a level of 4%-5% in 1928 and 1929. In more recent years, the jobless rate peaked at 7.5% in 1992 has been steadily declining since. In July, 1997, the unemployment rate stood at 4.8%, the lowest level in twenty-four years.

International Trade: Following World War I, the U.S. was a creditor nation. Many foreign countries, especially in Europe, owed the United States substantial sums due to War debts and to the trade surplus the country enjoyed at that time. In 1929, exports amounted to about 6-7% of GNP. Today, the U.S. is a debtor nation. Exports today are about 13% of GNP and there has been a balance of trade deficit. Moreover, much growth is expected to come from overseas, especially Asia, and these markets are not an "absolute certainty," by any means.

Stock Market Valuation: At the high in 1929, in current dollars, the total market value of all equities was close to $100 billion, about equal to the level of the country's Gross National Product that year and total federal debt was less than $20 billion. At this writing, the market value of all securities today is close to $10 trillion, GNP is between $7-$7.5 trillion, and the national debt is more than $5.5 trillion.

Relating equity values to gold prices is not totally appropriate since 1929 gold quotes were fixed at $20.67. However, given the deflationary environment of the day, it seems unlikely that gold prices would have been much different. At its 386.10 high in 1929, the Dow Jones Industrial Average was equivalent to 18.7 ounces of gold. At the recent 1997 high of 8340, the DJIA was valued at 25.7 ounces of gold which was, coincidentally, roughly the same relationship as the GNP ratio.

"Earnings Power"

In the late 1960's, and especially in the early 1970's, one of the favorite "buzz words" of the day was "earnings power." This term was born out of necessity in those go-go days because analysts desperately needed a "hook" to sell their "Nifty-Fifty" ideas to institutions.

Polaroid, for example, was constructing a new plant in Norwood to assemble its revolutionary "Aladdin" instant camera, later named the SX-70. Once the new facility was complete, millions of consumers would be buying film shipped from the new Waltham factory. When Polaroid hit 149 1/2 in May, 1972, the company's 1976 "earnings power" was being pegged by more "conservative" analysts at $4.00 per share. Forget that earnings would be down sharply in 1972 from the reported $1.86 per share of the year before. Without discussing Polaroid's "earnings power," who in his right mind would buy the stock at 100 times earnings?

It wasn't just Polaroid. Avon Products had an army of ladies knocking on doors! Xerox's Model 7000 duplicator revenues were projected to be greater than the size of the entire company ten years earlier; and Coca-Cola's purchase of Aqua-Chem raised hopes that drinking water could be made from the ocean.

Although it was lasciviously exploited in those days, the concept of "earnings power" is sound. Essentially what it offers is a "handle" on future values as companies grow into their existing abilities to produce. Of course, there can be interruptions to progress, such as war, recessions, oil embargos, or whatever. But it usually becomes necessary to build new plants, add new equipment, hire new salespeople, and so on, as a company moves from one stage to the next. Regardless of the reasons, the result is a step-like growth pattern for most companies. And this concept of "earnings power" can be applied to the market as well.

How does it work?

First, establish a valuation model. Using history as a guide, identify the growth phases and apply a price/earnings multiple "band" based on past and projected earnings. The longer the time period and the more data available, the better. The next page illustrates how the concept of earnings power was applied to an historic monthly chart of General Electric between 1942 and 1967.

The earnings growth phases were 1942 to 1945 (earnings per share rose from $0.52 to $0.65); 1946 to 1950 (earnings went from $0.50 to $2.00 per share); 1951 to 1954 ($1.60 to $2.46); 1955 to 1959 ($2.32 to $3.19); and 1960 to 1967 ($2.26 to $4.01 per share). Notice, too, that the stock "went parabolic" in 1953 and then dropped to just below the beginning of Stage IV (refer to the earlier explanation in Chapter 3).

General Electric's 26-year growth rate was 8.2% per year, which was a respectable showing since it was GE's policy to pay out roughly 70% of its earnings. (Obviously, GE's priorities have changed in more recent years.) Between 1942 and 1967, the high and low price/earnings multiples averaged 24.1 and 17.8 times, respectively, with 21 considered the "norm." If these multiples are applied to the "earnings power" at the end of each phase, a "band" of value is created, as shown on the chart.

There is one additional tool that can be extremely valuable whenever dividends are involved in the analysis. Question: How many years of future dividends are you buying at any given time? For instance, at GE's top in 1946, a buyer would be paying 12 years of future dividends. At the peak in 1957, it was 21 years; in 1959, 23 years; and at the high in 1965, it was 20 years of dividends. How do you calculate future unearned dividends?. Just apply the company's underlying growth rate to the most recent dividend paid. Again, the "future dividend stream" is but one more tool when you put the "earnings power" concept to work.

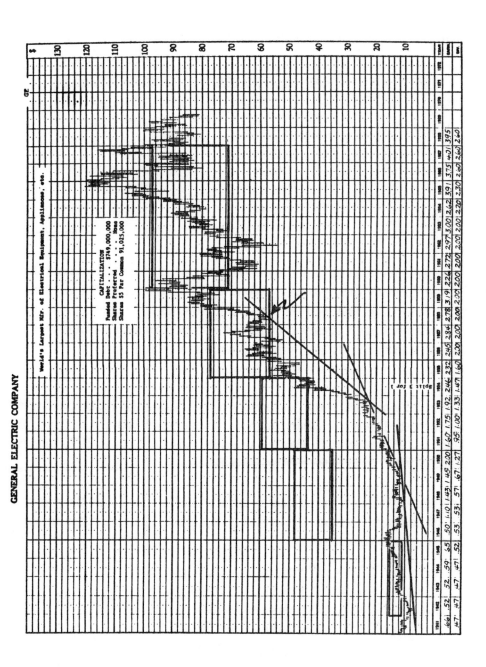

GENERAL ELECTRIC COMPANY

World's Largest Mfr. of Electrical Equipment, Appliances, etc.

CAPITALIZATION

Funded Debt $749,000,000
Shares Preferred . . . . None
Shares $5 Par Common 91,025,000

Next, let us apply the "earnings power" concept to the overall market...

GROWTH PHASE	EARNINGS POWER	YEARS OF FUTURE DIVIDENDS (Peaks)
1945 to 1950	30.70	15-17 years
1952 to 1957	36.08	18-22 years
1958 to 1966	57.68	22-24 years
1970 to 1974	99.04	17-20 years
1975 to 1979	124.46	14-17 years
1982 to 1989	221.48	13-18 years
1991 to 1998	440.00	17-24 years (estimated)

Due to the inclusion of a more contemporary list of companies into the Dow Industrials over the past several decades, a steady 40% dividend payout ratio was assumed for consistency on the table above. It would have been wrong to assume that the 60%+ payout ratios years ago would also be seen today, just as it might be wrong to assume today's 36% ratio will be continuing into the future as well.

It should be noted that the "earnings power" during the 1950 phase was not surpassed in any meaningful way for another 5 years; and it was 6 years in 1957; 6 years in 1966; 4 years in 1974; 8 years in 1979; and 5 years in 1989. Also, refer to Appendix B.

Another way to view the preceding table would be to measure the growth rate of earnings from one cycle peak to the next. Here are those figures for the past 48 years:

1950 to 1957	(7 years):	2.3% per year
1957 to 1966	(9 years):	5.4% " "
1966 to 1974	(8 years):	7.0% " "
1974 to 1979	(5 years):	4.7% " "
1979 to 1989	(10 years):	6.1% " "
1989 to 1998	(9 years):	7.8% " " (author estimate)

Notice that the growth rate in recent years is better than at any other time. This accounts for much of today's optimism.

Lately, Wall Street observers have been proclaiming, "Good news! The business cycle has been repealed!" You will also hear the comment, "This time it's different!" Remember, these were the very same comments made during the Spring of 1929. Maybe this time it is, indeed, different. However, judging by the experiences of the past fifty years, there is no way to be sure.

When reading the earlier tables as well as the next chart, you should apply a personal estimate to the future rather than merely accepting the 440 earnings projection furnished here. Conditions and estimates can change. And opinions can differ. For example, if the current cycle is expected to last longer and go higher, and a 490 "earnings power" is assumed for 1999 instead, the band would become 7350 (high) and 5880 (low).

Corporate profits will always be the long term key to future stock prices and a proper assessment of the earnings trend and the rate of growth are instrumental for success in the stock market. Today's investors have discovered that an environment of low interest rates and low inflation can help buoy stock values. However, as every investor in 1930 learned, low interest rates and low inflation do *not*, by themselves, lead to higher stock prices. For this reason, calculating "earnings power" is a worthwhile and recommended analytical exercise and while the entire approach is, admittedly, very subjective, it can provide some needed perspective to individual stocks and to the market in general.

Finally, let us see how the "earnings power" figures appear on a chart of the Dow Jones Inustrial Average since World War II. The growth periods identified for the Dow are illustrated as follows:

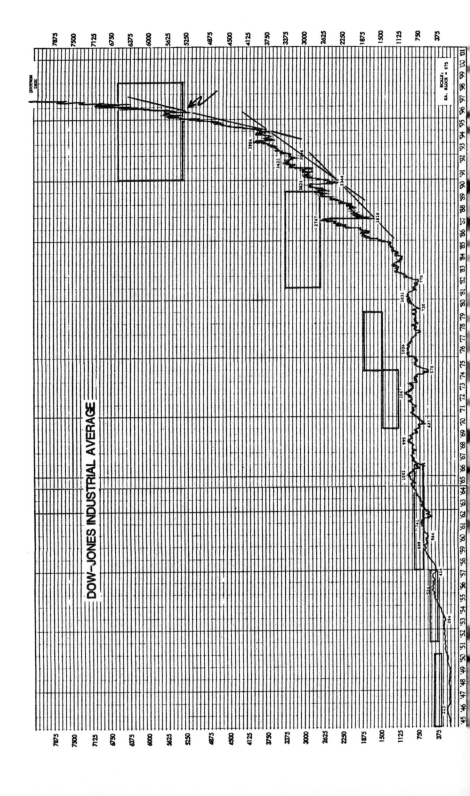

DOW-JONES INDUSTRIAL AVERAGE

CHAPTER EIGHT
MONEY INFLOWS INTO THE STOCK MARKET

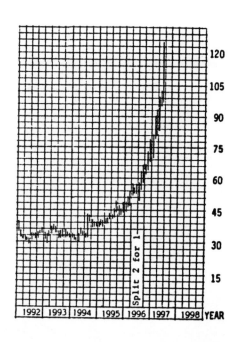

Money Inflows Into The Stock Market

The Demographics

There is absolutely no doubt about it! The Stock Market will be recorded in history as *the* story of the nineties. Clearly, stocks have become the savings vehicle of choice for an entire generation of investors as they prepare for retirement.

This population group has shaped the entire economy from one decade to the next. When annual births climbed from about 2.9 million just after World War II to 4.3 million per year well into the 1950's, the so-called "baby-boomers" had arrived.

From then on, their impact would be significant — on housing and household formations in the 1950's, on schools in the 1960's, on colleges in the 1970's, on employment and consumption in the 1980's, and on money, savings, and investing in the 1990's.

The huge sums going into the stock market every month are now a regular topic in the evening financial report. Most investment advisors expect IRA, 401(k) and other retirement funds to be flowing into the market in generous quantities well into the new century. Those born in 1946 will turn 65 in the year 2011, so people see little reason to be concerned that this inflow of money will end anytime soon. This is, in fact, the principal argument in favor of higher stock prices for the next few years and a continuation of THE GREAT INDEX MANIA.

How can any analyst question such a powerful demographic trend? Well, there is one angle observers could be overlooking, and it might impact future corporate revenues and earnings...

For most people, reaching the 35-to-40 age bracket marks a milestone of sorts. At this point, they have learned their trade and they are highly productive workers, their earnings are soaring, and they can be called prime consumers in almost every respect. This age category might even constitute the single most important contributing group to the overall economy.

If this is so, it should be noted that the 35-40 age group is larger today than at any time in history — over 40% larger than fifteen years ago when the bull market started its great climb! It should also be noted that the number in this group will be shrinking substantially beginning in 1998 — about 10% over the next several years. This significant demographic shift could hinder corporate profits in the 1998-2004 period the same way it helped in years past. Clearly, the "baby-boomers" have been in their most productive and most consumptive stages over the past fifteen years. That is about to end.

Yet, in lemming fashion, the money pours in. In mid-1997, assets of U.S. stock funds exceeded $2 trillion for the first time in history, up from almost $200 billion ten years earlier. At year-end 1996, the assets of all funds totaled $3.5 trillion (up about 25% from 1995). Of this, stock funds accounted for $1.7 trillion; money market funds, $900 billion; and bond funds $900 billion. Also, 1996 saw record inflows of more than $225 billion into stock funds, or an average of almost $19 billion each month.

A skeptic will argue that, ultimately, the *long term fundamentals* will dictate the value of investments — not the money chasing them over the short term. A skeptic will also warn that any sudden change in sentiment would almost certainly result in a swift and ferocious return to more traditional valuations — especially if earnings prove disappointing. If the stock market peaks thirty-six years after the "baby-boomer" birth rate peaked (ie., 1998), the same way it began in 1982, there could be fewer millionaires in 2011 than many now expect.

The Index Funds

Vanguard's Index 500 Portfolio, a no-load fund, is already one of the largest stock funds today with assets approaching $40 billion. The fact that Vanguard's equity funds were taking in more than 10% of all inflows to stock funds during the first half of 1997 makes them a major factor in this area. Also, Fidelity, another industry powerhouse, has recently announced the creation of still more index-oriented funds.

In addition to the new index funds created in recent years and the "pseudo" index funds mentioned earlier, there is yet another force in this market—the Standard & Poor's Depository Receipts, or SPDRs, traded on the American Stock Exchange. Created in 1993, and administered by SPDR Service Corp, a unit of the AMEX, the SPDR is also based on the S&P 500 Index and trades more than two million shares each day. As such, it is frequently the most active issue traded on the AMEX.

Unlike index funds, SPDRs do not reinvest dividends automatically as most investors prefer. Instead, dividends are paid to the shareholders quarterly. However, SPDRs are especially popular because they can be bought or sold (even sold short), although not commission-free, any time during the trading day, while fund orders are executed at 4 p.m., either the same day or the next.

Supply & Demand

To say the Dow Jones Industrial Average has done well over the past fifteen years would be an understatement. Since 1982, the Average has advanced at an annual clip of 17% per year, including a 33% gain in 1995, a 26% increase in 1996, and more of the same in 1997. This is an incredible return from companies growing at a much slower rate. A 20% rate suggests that any patient investor can make TEN TIMES his or her original capital every thirteen years. Can this continue over the long term? Of course not.

There's an old Wall Street joke that goes something like this:

When Sam, the broker, called his client, he said: "I've run across an interesting situation, Marvin. The stock is now $20 and it appears headed for $30 over the near term."

"That sounds great! Buy 500 shares at the market," Marvin said.

A week later, Sam spoke with his client again and said: "It's now $30 and it has the potential to go to $50! Did you want me to enter that order to buy more?"

"Absolutely!," Marvin said enthusiastically. "Buy more at the market!"

When Sam called his client a few weeks later, he said: "Marvin, the stock is now $50. Do you want to buy any more?"

"No," said his client. "Instead, I think it's time to take profits. Sell it ALL at the market, Sam!"

"Sell?," exclaimed Sam. "To whom?"

Is there anyone reading this who has not played the game "Old Maid?" Or "Snap?" Or "Musical Chairs?" The GREAT INDEX MANIA, which began in earnest in late 1994, is now beginning to resemble such a game.

Will the "baby-boomers" who are expecting to "cash out" their hard-earned gains in the years ahead find it more difficult when the demographic shift, as explained earlier, comes into play? That might be the case. And if they all suddenly decide to cash out at the same time, the "land of milk and honey" may prove to be only an illusion.

CHAPTER NINE
BEFORE AND AFTER THE CRASH

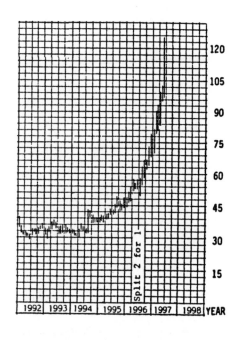

Before and After the Crash

Avoiding a stock market crash before it occurs is, by far, the best way to "profit" from it. Whenever investment dollars can be reinvested buying substantially more at much lower prices than what was sold, the investor has profited. In the meantime, here are a few common-sense suggestions to be better informed and to avoid becoming "trapped" when the bubble bursts:

SEEK MAXIMUM FLEXIBILITY

The single most important objective should be to protect your investment principal whenever the risk of losing it is high. It is wrong to assume the value of any portfolio, no matter how high its quality, will continue to grow simply because there could be "more buyers than sellers." The "greater fool theory" has never been known to hold up stock prices for an extended period of time.

Place your investment dollars only into vehicles that permit you to quickly and easily switch into other, safer places when you think it is necessary. A measly 3% or 5% return, even for an extended period, is far better than a 40%+ loss that may not be recovered for five or ten years. Moreover, if prices do fall, your capital will be available for reinvestment at more reasonable valuations.

Some company-sponsored 401(k) plans allow money shifts only two times in any single year, so it is very important that these opportunities not be squandered.

Mutual fund holders should favor any investment group or "family" that offers an ability to switch freely at little or no cost from its equity fund, for example, into its money market fund, or into its bond fund, or whatever.

Unfortunately, as one would expect, many fund organizations discourage money shifts and have deliberately created annoying obstacles for fund holders, making it even more necessary for investors to study the "fine print" before committing new money.

DEVISE AN "ASSET ALLOCATION" PLAN

Prepare a "battle plan" that involves shifting your assets when you are especially uneasy. In its simplest form, your holdings should be divided between equities, bonds, and a cash reserve. For example, an 80%-15%-5% split would, for most people, be regarded as "bullish," while a 20%-35%-45% allocation mix could be viewed as quite "bearish." Although every investor is different, having a basic plan is a good idea. This is analogous to being certain the building you are in has a fire escape.

Also, in this regard, here is a reminder. Money Market Funds, which have become very popular since they were first organized in the early 1970's, now account for about $1 trillion of total fund assets. However, they can fluctuate in value and, unlike bank accounts, they are not insured by the FDIC.

LEARN MORE ABOUT YOUR INVESTMENTS

If your retirement funds are invested in a mutual fund, learn more about its largest holdings. Check a copy of *Understanding Wall Street*, Third Edition, from your public library and examine these stocks and assess their risks carefully.

In addition, you should be comfortable discussing the subjects of this book and challenging or agreeing with those who are debating its points. Whether you agree or disagree with the message here, ignorance should not be an excuse if a substantial portion of your capital is lost simply because a stock market debacle occurred "that no one could foresee."

KNOW THE TAX CONSEQUENCES

Discuss the tax consequences of any changes you could be making to your portfolios the next time you consult with a CPA or an expert who can answer questions of this type. In addition, explore how the recent changes to the capital gains tax might affect you today and in the future.

STUDY INDEX FUNDS FROM THE INSIDE

Contact Vanguard, Fidelity and other index fund managers to learn more about them through their literature. Although the big-cap stocks appear overvalued at this writing, they won't always be. Contact Vanguard Group by calling (800) 662-7447 and Fidelity at (800) 544-8888. Also, learn more about the SPDR (ticker symbol SPY) on the American Stock Exchange. The AMEX is located at 86 Trinity Place in New York City.

MAKE 'EM PROVE IT

When a mutual fund manager or salesperson offers facts, figures, and charts about the "growth" of a fund, ask about the fund's holdings. How the fund has performed over the past year (or five years) is important, of course. However, the underlying earnings growth of the stocks held in the fund and the average P/E of the portfolio are no less important. When they talk "performance," make 'em prove it by asking them for details beyond how rapidly the fund's net asset value (NAV) has risen compared with the S&P 500.

One contrary approach to THE GREAT INDEX MANIA is what advisors call "value-investing." This form of stock selection has been popular for a long time. It has its advocates and many funds favor this approach. Unfortunately, portfolios of this type often feature companies that have special problems, or they are burdened with additional risks for one reason or another. However, value-investing should not be dismissed altogether. As before, "make 'em prove it" by inquiring about the earnings prospects for the companies in the portfolio.

LEARN MORE ABOUT STOCK OPTIONS

Conservative investors and those who prefer to leave the details of investing to others need not be concerned with this section. On the other hand, investors able to tolerate a greater degree of risk are advised to explore one particular avenue of stock options: *writing covered calls*. Otherwise, stock options are not recommended for those seeking "capital preservation."

Read the "Stock Options" chapter in *Understanding Wall Street* to learn about options and how they work.

Writing covered calls is an ideal tool for any investor who *already owns a stock and is not afraid to sell it*. Other than being forced to sell your shares at a predetermined price, there is little risk by writing (selling) a covered call against stock already held in your portfolio. When a call is written against a "long" position, increased income can be obtained simply by granting another person the right (an option) to buy the stock from you at a predetermined price (the "strike price"), within a predetermined time limit (the "term"). Ask your investment advisor for additional details and an explanation of the tax consequences.

BE PREPARED AND READY TO ACT

By building a "library" of useful information and background material on companies, funds, and other subjects, you will have information available when you need it. Also, if a stock market crash occurred tomorrow, realistically, what would you like to buy and at what price? Answer this question and you have your "approved list." Concentrate on stocks (or fund portfolios of such) that offer these two characteristics as a minimum: First, favor companies that are well-established in stable, growing industries with solid balance sheets (low debt and high levels of cash). Second, look for companies that will be increasing sales and earnings at not less than 12%-15% annually for at least five years into the future. Monitor these potential investments and update this "approved" list on a regular basis.

After the Crash

The next bear market will almost certainly be more severe than the one that occurred in 1987 for several reasons:

1. Although stock prices were high in 1987, a "mania" was not present as it is today.

2. In 1987, buybacks were done primarily as a defensive (price support) measure. Today, buybacks are being used to raise earnings per share, as a way to shrink the supply of stock available for sale, and, in part, as a method of holding down employment costs. In short, companies today are using investors' equity to speculate in the stock market.

3. Unlike 1987, U.S. demographic trends in the future will be much less favorable to corporate profits.

4. Corporate earnings were not a major concern and companies were confident profits would not collapse in 1987. Cost reduction measures to maintain profit margins could have been put in place if necessary. Today, much of that has already happened.

5. Moreso today than any other time in the past, billions of dollars are being invested professionally by young portfolio managers who

have never experienced a major bear market. Also, the "public" was less involved and less concerned with the stock market years ago. There is much more at stake today and a major setback will be quite emotional for most investors.

Some experts believe if a serious price decline does occur, 401(k) and other retirement money will continue to flow into the market without interruption creating a gradual erosion similar to the 1972-74 experience. There is some merit to this argument. However, the "mania" and the parabolic nature of the stock charts suggest otherwise.

Needless to say, the investment environment after any crash will depend to a large extent on the reasons for it in the first place. The scenario outlined on the next page is based on a shift in the economic fortunes of the nation due to demographics for the most part. The implied result is deflationary with corporate profits coming under some pressure. However, if one adds the (not-so-impossible) occurence of another oil embargo similar to the early 1970's, as an example, then the expected economic landscape changes dramatically. Predicting unforseen events is not an easy task, making it all the more necessary for today's investor to remain vigilant and to have a grasp of "the big picture."

> *"It's a rare person who wants to hear*
> *what he doesn't want to hear."*
> *- Dick Cavett*

After the crash, expect to see the following:

1. Corporate bond yields will climb substantially to probably 8% to 10% or higher. Also, company bankruptcies and mergers will be announced often.

2. Price/earnings ratios will be considerably lower than today. Look for a P/E ratio of roughly 12 times the "earnings power" of the DJIA, reflecting competition from bonds and the prospects or reality of lower corporate profits. Maintain a faith that the DJIA earnings will be growing about 7% annually longer term.

3. Yields on government bonds will probably remain steady at the 3-4% level.

4. Stock prices will not be returning to their earlier highs for many years.

5. The prices for homes, real estate, and other "hard assets" will be falling and there will be a great demand for currency.

6. The unemployment rate will climb sharply.

7. The government deficit will begin climbing again due to public demands for more government spending to "stimulate" the economy.

Eventually, quality stocks will be available to those investors who have the capital and fortitude to commit to a very nervous and very discouraged stock market. Do not try to catch the exact lows. Instead, invest cautiously. Time will be on the side of those who hold cash. And those investors who understand the fundamentals and the reasons it happened will be in control. Once the dust settles, earnings growth, yields, balance sheet analysis, and other proven means of judging value will again be in vogue.

Conclusion

Recently, the Standard & Poor's 500 Index vaulted over 950 and the Dow Jones Industrials passed 8300 for the first time. Both have more than doubled from late-1994 levels. Will the Dow reach 9,000 any time soon? Or maybe 12,000? Unfortunately, the precise answer cannot be found in this book. However, you now have a better understanding of stock market crashes and know what to expect. Hopefully, this book will help you avoid the next debacle and enjoy more prosperous years after it occurs.

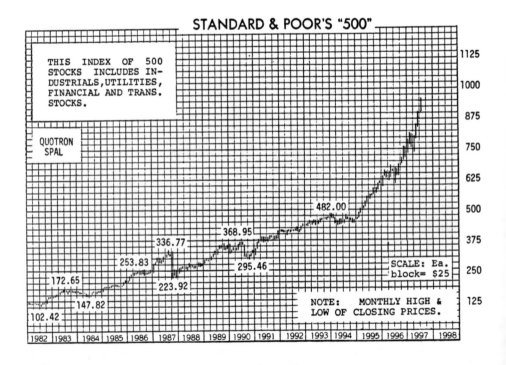

STANDARD & POOR'S "500"

THIS INDEX OF 500 STOCKS INCLUDES INDUSTRIALS, UTILITIES, FINANCIAL AND TRANS. STOCKS.

QUOTRON SPAL

SCALE: Ea. block= $25

NOTE: MONTHLY HIGH & LOW OF CLOSING PRICES.

APPENDIX A

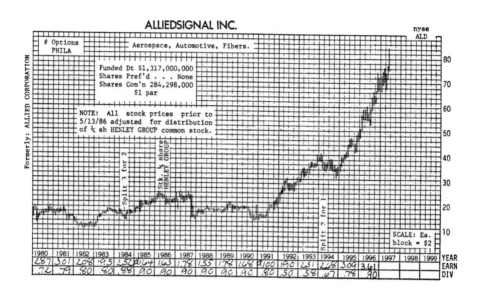

ALLIEDSIGNAL INC.

nyse
ALD

Options
PHILA

Aerospace, Automotive, Fibers.

Formerly: ALLIED CORPORATION

Funded Dt $1,317,000,000
Shares Pref'd . . . None
Shares Com'n 284,298,000
$1 par

NOTE: All stock prices prior to
5/13/86 adjusted for distribution
of ½ sh HENLEY GROUP common stock.

Split 3 for 2

Stk. ½ share
HENLEY GROUP

Split 2 for 1

SCALE: Ea.
block = $2

YEAR	1980	1981	1982	1983	1984	1985	1986	1987	1988	1989	1990	1991	1992	1993	1994	1995	1996	1997	1998	1999
EARN	2.87	3.01	2.08	⁹.5	2.52	2.64	1.63	1.78	1.55	1.78	1.68	2.00	1.90	2.31	2.68	3.09	3.61			
DIV	.72	.79	.80	.80	.88	.90	.90	.90	.90	.90	.90	.80	.50	.58	.67	.78	.90			

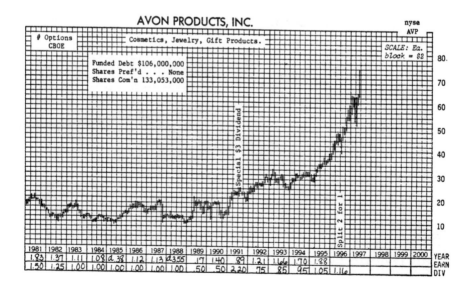

AVON PRODUCTS, INC.

nyse
AVP

Options
CBOE

Cosmetics, Jewelry, Gift Products.

SCALE: Ea.
block = $2

Funded Debt $106,000,000
Shares Pref'd . . . None
Shares Com'n 133,053,000

Special $3 Dividend

Split 2 for 1

YEAR	1981	1982	1983	1984	1985	1986	1987	1988	1989	1990	1991	1992	1993	1994	1995	1996	1997	1998	1999	2000
EARN	1.83	1.37	1.11	1.08	d.38	1.12	1.13	d3.55	.17	1.40	.89	1.21	1.66	1.70	1.88					
DIV	1.50	1.25	1.00	1.00	1.00	1.00	1.00	1.00	.50	.50	2.20	.75	.85	.95	1.05	1.16				

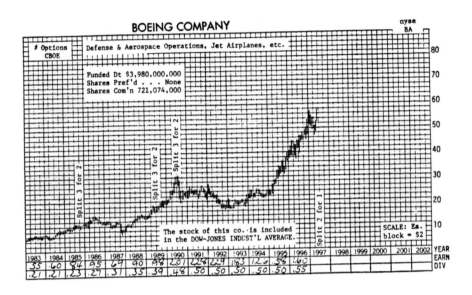

BOEING COMPANY   nyse
                                                        BA

Options
CBOE   Defense & Aerospace Operations, Jet Airplanes, etc.

            Funded Dt $3,980,000,000
            Shares Pref'd . . . None
            Shares Com'n 721,074,000

The stock of this co. is included
in the DOW-JONES INDUST'L AVERAGE.

SCALE: Ea.
block = $2

YEAR	1983	1984	1985	1986	1987	1988	1989	1990	1991	1992	1993	1994	1995	1996	1997	1998	1999	2000	2001	2002
EARN	55	60	84	95	69	90	98	2.01	2.28	2.29	1.83	1.26	58	1.60						
DIV	.21	.21	.23	.27	.31	.35	.39	.48	.50	.50	.50	.50	.50	.55						

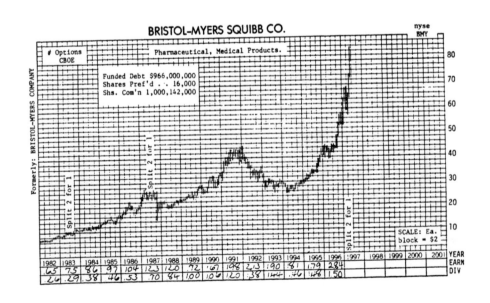

BRISTOL-MYERS SQUIBB CO.   nyse
                                                        BMY

Options
CBOE   Pharmaceutical, Medical Products.

            Funded Debt $966,000,000
            Shares Pref'd . . 16,000
            Shs. Com'n 1,000,142,000

Formerly: BRISTOL-MYERS COMPANY

SCALE: Ea.
block = $2

YEAR	1982	1983	1984	1985	1986	1987	1988	1989	1990	1991	1992	1993	1994	1995	1996	1997	1998	1999	2000	2001
EARN	65	75	86	97	104	1.23	1.20	72	1.67	1.98	2.13	1.90	81	1.79	2.84					
DIV	26	.29	.38	.46	.53	.70	.84	1.00	1.06	1.20	.38	1.44	.76	1.48	1.50					

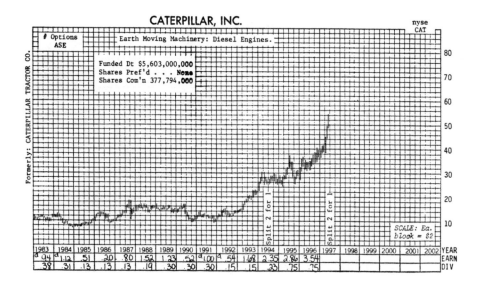

CATERPILLAR, INC.

nyse
CAT

Options ASE

Earth Moving Machinery: Diesel Engines.

Formerly: CATERPILLAR TRACTOR CO.

Funded Dt $5,603,000,000
Shares Pref'd . . . None
Shares Com'n 377,794,000

Split 2 for 1

Split 2 for 1

SCALE: Ea.
block = $2

YEAR	1983	1984	1985	1986	1987	1988	1989	1990	1991	1992	1993	1994	1995	1996	1997	1998	1999	2000	2001	2002
EARN	d.94	d1.12	.51	.20	.80	1.52	1.23	.52	d1.00	d.54	1.68	2.35	2.86	3.54						
DIV	.38	.31	.13	.13	.13	.19	.30	.30	.30	.15	.15	.23	.75	.75						

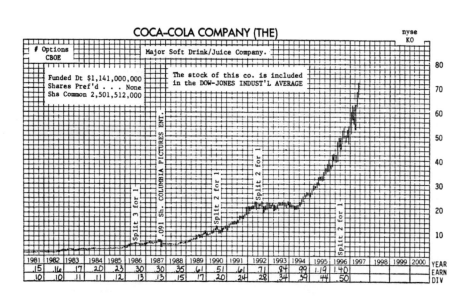

COCA-COLA COMPANY (THE)

nyse
KO

Options CBOE

Major Soft Drink/Juice Company.

Funded Dt $1,141,000,000
Shares Pref'd . . . None
Shs Common 2,501,512,000

The stock of this co. is included
in the DOW-JONES INDUST'L AVERAGE

Split 3 for 1

.091 Sh. COLUMBIA PICTURES ENT.

Split 2 for 1

Split 2 for 1

Split 2 for 1

YEAR	1981	1982	1983	1984	1985	1986	1987	1988	1989	1990	1991	1992	1993	1994	1995	1996	1997	1998	1999	2000
EARN	.15	.16	.17	.20	.23	.30	.30	.35	.61	.51	.61	.71	.84	.99	1.19	1.40				
DIV	.10	.10	.11	.11	.12	.13	.13	.15	.17	.20	.24	.28	.34	.39	.44	.50				

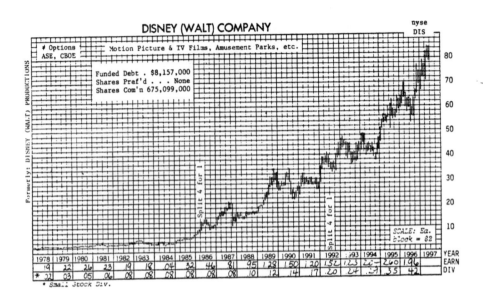

DISNEY (WALT) COMPANY

nyse
DIS

Formerly: DISNEY (WALT) PRODUCTIONS

Options
ASE, CBOE

Motion Picture & TV Films, Amusement Parks, etc.

Funded Debt . $8,157,000
Shares Pref'd . . . None
Shares Com'n 675,099,000

Split 4 for 1
Split 4 for 1
Split 4 for 1

SCALE: Ea.
block = $2

YEAR	1978	1979	1980	1981	1982	1983	1984	1985	1986	1987	1988	1989	1990	1991	1992	'93	1994	1995	1996	1997
EARN	19	22	26	23	19	18	.04	32	46	81	95	128	150	20	152	125	20	260	196	
DIV	.02	.03	.05	.06	.08	.08	.08	.08	.08	.08	.10	.12	.14	.17	.20	.24	.29	.35	.42	

* Small Stock Div.

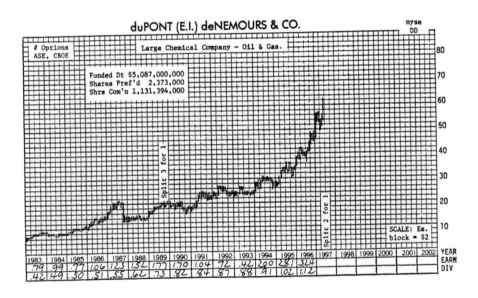

duPONT (E.I.) deNEMOURS & CO.

nyse
DD

Options
ASE, CBOE

Large Chemical Company - Oil & Gas.

Funded Dt $5,087,000,000
Shares Pref'd 2,373,000
Shrs Com'n 1,131,394,000

Split 3 for 1
Split 2 for 1

SCALE: Ea.
block = $2

YEAR	1983	1984	1985	1986	1987	1988	1989	1990	1991	1992	1993	1994	1995	1996	1997	1998	1999	2000	2001	2002
EARN	.79	.99	.77	1.06	1.23	1.52	1.77	1.70	1.04	72	.42	2.90	2.81	3.24						
DIV	.42	.49	.50	.51	.55	.62	.73	.82	.84	.87	.88	.91	1.02	1.12						

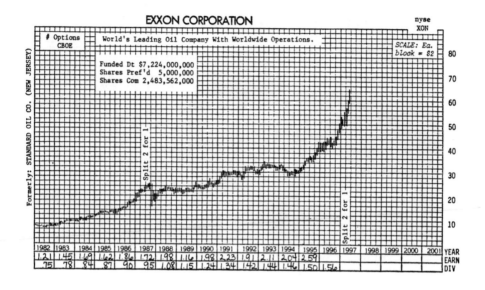

EXXON CORPORATION

nyse
XON

Options CBOE

World's Leading Oil Company With Worldwide Operations.

SCALE: Ea. block = $2

Funded Dt $7,224,000,000
Shares Pref'd 5,000,000
Shares Com 2,483,562,000

Formerly: STANDARD OIL CO. (NEW JERSEY)

Split 2 for 1

Split 2 for 1

	1982	1983	1984	1985	1986	1987	1988	1989	1990	1991	1992	1993	1994	1995	1996	1997	1998	1999	2000	2001	YEAR
EARN	1.21	1.45	1.69	1.62	1.86	1.72	1.98	1.16	1.98	2.23	1.91	2.11	2.04	2.59							
DIV	.75	.78	.84	.87	.90	.95	1.08	1.15	1.24	1.34	1.42	1.44	1.46	1.50	1.56						

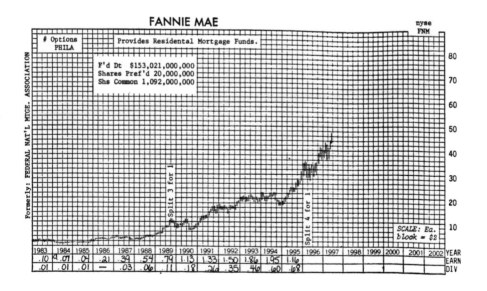

FANNIE MAE

nyse
FNM

Options PHILA

Provides Residental Mortgage Funds.

F'd Dt $153,021,000,000
Shares Pref'd 20,000,000
Shs Common 1,092,000,000

Formerly: FEDERAL NAT'L MTGE. ASSOCIATION

Split 3 for 1

Split 4 for 1

SCALE: Ea. block = $2

	1983	1984	1985	1986	1987	1988	1989	1990	1991	1992	1993	1994	1995	1996	1997	1998	1999	2000	2001	2002	YEAR
EARN	.10	d.01	.09	.21	.39	.54	.79	1.13	1.33	1.50	1.86	1.95	1.16								
DIV	.01	.01	.01	—	.03	.06	.11	.18	.26	.35	.46	.60	.68								

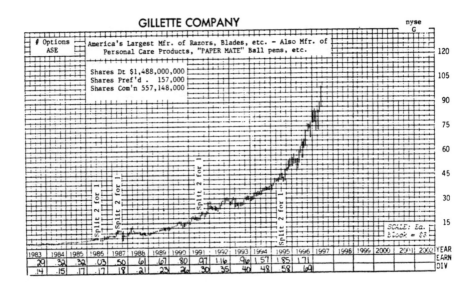

GILLETTE COMPANY

Options
ASE

America's Largest Mfr. of Razors, Blades, etc. - Also Mfr. of
Personal Care Products, "PAPER MATE" Ball pens, etc.

Shares Dt $1,488,000,000
Shares Pref'd . 157,000
Shares Com'n 557,148,000

nyse
G

SCALE: Ea.
block = $3

YEAR	1983	1984	1985	1986	1987	1988	1989	1990	1991	1992	1993	1994	1995	1996	1997	1998	1999	2000	2001	2002
EARN	29	32	32	.03	.50	61	.67	80	97	1.16	96	1.57	1.85	1.71						
DIV	.14	.15	.17	.17	18	.21	23	26	30	35	40	48	58	69						

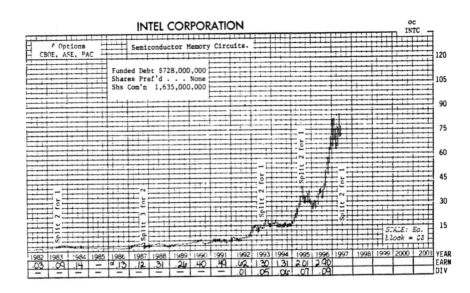

INTEL CORPORATION

Options
CBOE, ASE, PAC

Semiconductor Memory Circuits.

Funded Debt $728,000,000
Shares Pref'd . . . None
Shs Com'n 1,635,000,000

oc
INTC

SCALE: Ea.
block = $3

YEAR	1982	1983	1984	1985	1986	1987	1988	1989	1990	1991	1992	1993	1994	1995	1996	1997	1998	1999	2000	2001
EARN	.03	.09	.14	—	d.13	.12	.31	.26	40	49	.62	1.30	1.31	2.01	2.90					
DIV	—	—	—	—	—	—	—	—	—	—	.01	.05	.06	.07	.09					

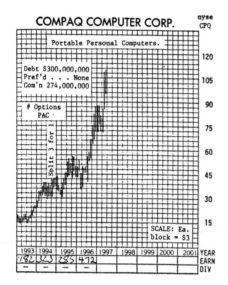

COMPAQ COMPUTER CORP. nyse CPQ

Portable Personal Computers.

Debt $300,000,000
Pref'd . . . None
Com'n 274,000,000

Options
PAC

Split 3 for 1

SCALE: Ea. block = $3

120
105
90
75
60
45
30
15

1993	1994	1995	1996	1997	1998	1999	2000	2001	YEAR
1.82	3.23	2.85	4.72						EARN
—	—	—	—						DIV

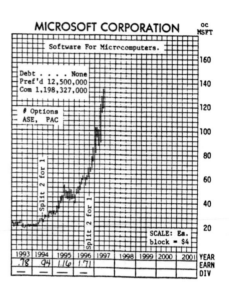

MICROSOFT CORPORATION oc MSFT

Software For Microcomputers.

Debt . . . . None
Pref'd 12,500,000
Com 1,198,327,000

Options
ASE, PAC

Split 2 for 1
Split 2 for 1

SCALE: Ea. block = $4

160
140
120
100
80
60
40
20

1993	1994	1995	1996	1997	1998	1999	2000	2001	YEAR
.78	.94	1.16	1.71						EARN
—	—	—	—						DIV

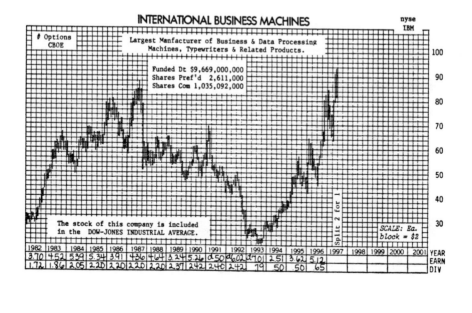

INTERNATIONAL BUSINESS MACHINES nyse IBM

Options
CBOE

Largest Manfacturer of Business & Data Processing
Machines, Typewriters & Related Products.

Funded Dt $9,669,000,000
Shares Pref'd 2,611,000
Shares Com 1,035,092,000

Split 2 for 1

The stock of this company is included
in the DOW-JONES INDUSTRIAL AVERAGE.

SCALE: Ea. block = $2

100
90
80
70
60
50
40
30

1982	1983	1984	1985	1986	1987	1988	1989	1990	1991	1992	1993	1994	1995	1996	1997	1998	1999	2000	2001	YEAR
3.70	4.52	5.39	5.34	3.91	4.36	4.64	3.24	5.26	d.50	d6.02	d7.01	2.51	3.62	5.12						EARN
1.72	1.86	2.05	2.20	2.20	2.20	2.20	2.37	2.42	2.40	2.42	.79	.50	.50	.65						DIV

MERCK & COMPANY

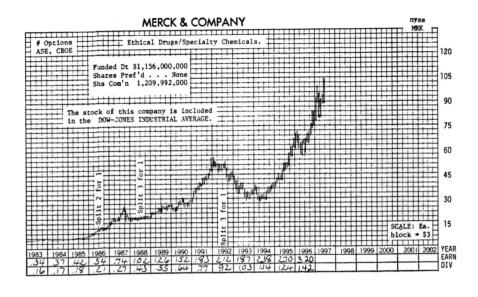

MERRILL LYNCH & CO., INC.

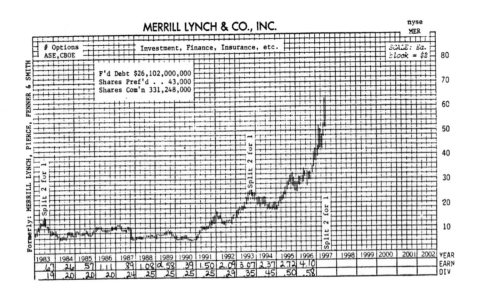

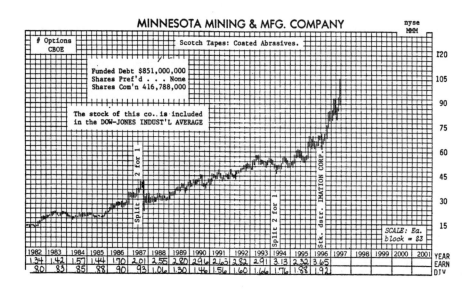

MINNESOTA MINING & MFG. COMPANY

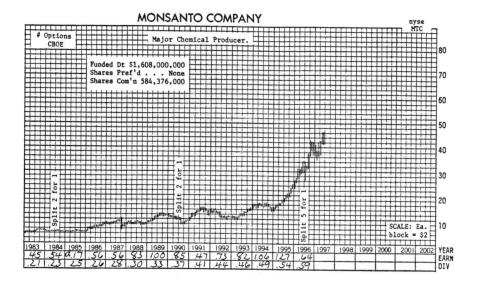

MONSANTO COMPANY

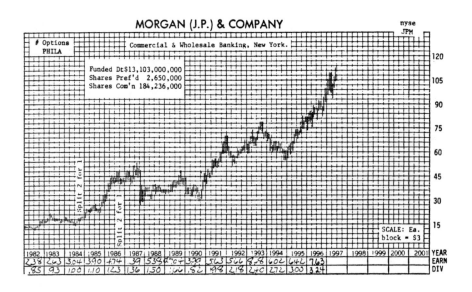

MORGAN (J.P.) & COMPANY

nyse
JPM

Options
PHILA

Commercial & Wholesale Banking, New York.

Funded Dt $13,103,000,000
Shares Pref'd 2,650,000
Shares Com'n 184,236,000

SCALE: Ea.
block = $3

YEAR	1982	1983	1984	1985	1986	1987	1988	1989	1990	1991	1992	1993	1994	1995	1996	1997	1998	1999	2000	2001
EARN	2.38	2.63	3.04	3.90	4.74	3.9	5.33	4.70+	3.99	5.63	5.66	8.8	6.02	6.42	7.63					
DIV	.85	.93	1.00	1.10	1.23	1.36	1.50	:.00	.82	.98	2.18	2.40	2.72	3.00	3.24					

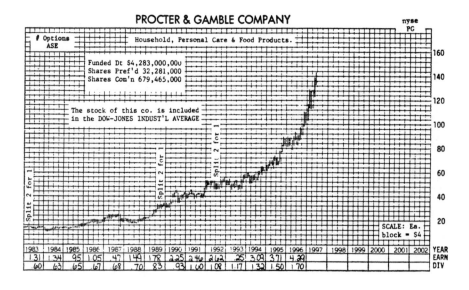

PROCTER & GAMBLE COMPANY

nyse
PG

Options
ASE

Household, Personal Care & Food Products.

Funded Dt $4,283,000,000
Shares Pref'd 32,281,000
Shares Com'n 679,465,000

The stock of this co. is included
in the DOW-JONES INDUST'L AVERAGE

SCALE: Ea.
block = $4

YEAR	1983	1984	1985	1986	1987	1988	1989	1990	1991	1992	1993	1994	1995	1996	1997	1998	1999	2000	2001	2002
EARN	1.31	1.34	.95	1.05	.47	1.49	1.78	2.25	2.46	2.62	.25	3.09	3.71	4.29						
DIV	.60	.63	.65	.67	.68	.70	.83	.93	1.00	1.08	1.17	1.32	1.50	1.70						

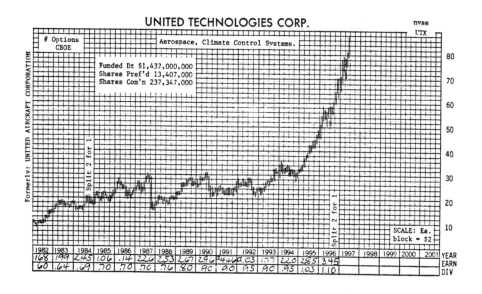

UNITED TECHNOLOGIES CORP.

nyse
UTX

Options
CBOE

Aerospace, Climate Control Systems.

Formerly: UNITED AIRCRAFT CORPORATION

Funded Dt $1,437,000,000
Shares Pref'd 13,407,000
Shares Com'n 237,347,000

Split 2 for 1

Split 2 for 1

SCALE: Ea.
block = $2

YEAR	1982	1983	1984	1985	1986	1987	1988	1989	1990	1991	1992	1993	1994	1995	1996	1997	1998	1999	2000	2001
EARN	1.68	1.99	2.45	1.06	.14	2.26	2.53	2.67	2.96	4.46	2.03	1.77	2.20	2.85	3.45					
DIV	.60	.64	.69	.70	.70	.70	.76	.80	.90	.90	.95	.90	.95	1.03	1.10					

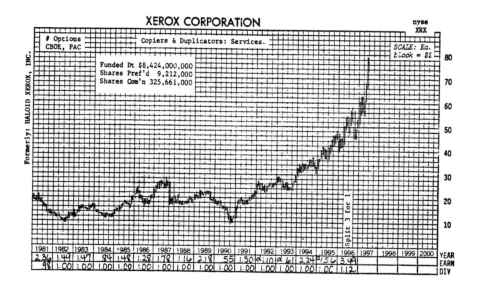

XEROX CORPORATION

nyse
XRX

Options
CBOE, PAC

Copiers & Duplicators: Services.

SCALE: Ea.
block = $2

Formerly: HALOID XEROX, INC.

Funded Dt $8,424,000,000
Shares Pref'd 9,212,000
Shares Com'n 325,661,000

Split 3 for 1

YEAR	1981	1982	1983	1984	1985	1986	1987	1988	1989	1990	1991	1992	1993	1994	1995	1996	1997	1998	1999	2000
EARN	2.36	1.49	1.47	.84	1.48	1.28	1.78	1.16	2.18	.55	1.30	d1.10	d.61	2.24	d1.56	3.40				
DIV	.98	1.00	1.00	1.00	1.00	1.00	1.00	1.00	1.00	1.00	1.00	1.00	1.00	1.00	.90	1.12				

APPENDIX B

SELECTED STATISTICS

	DJIA Close	DJIA Earnings	DJIA Divs	Payout Ratio	Avg. P/E	Div. Yield	Yrs. of Divs at the High	% Chg CPI
1945	193	10.56	6.69	63%	16.4	3.9%	17 yrs	-
1946	177	13.63	7.50	55%	13.8	4.0%	18 yrs	10.8%
1947	181	18.80	9.21	49%	9.3	5.3%	16 yrs	14.4%
1948	177	23.07	11.50	50%	7.8	6.4%	15 yrs	7.8%
1949	200	23.54	12.79	54%	7.7	7.0%	15 yrs	-1.0%
1950	235	30.70	16.13	53%	7.0	7.5%	17 yrs	1.0%
1951	269	26.59	16.34	61%	9.7	6.3%	18 yrs	7.9%
1952	292	24.78	15.43	62%	11.1	5.6%	18 yrs	2.2%
1953	281	27.23	16.11	59%	10.1	5.9%	18 yrs	0.8%
1954	404	28.18	17.47	62%	12.1	5.1%	20 yrs	0.5%
1955	488	35.78	21.58	60%	12.2	4.9%	22 yrs	0.4%
1956	499	33.34	22.99	69%	14.7	4.7%	22 yrs	1.5%
1957	436	36.08	21.61	60%	13.0	4.6%	22 yrs	3.6%
1958	584	27.95	20.00	72%	18.3	3.9%	22 yrs	2.7%
1959	679	34.31	20.74	60%	18.3	3.3%	23 yrs	0.8%
1960	616	32.21	21.36	66%	19.4	3.4%	23 yrs	1.6%
1961	731	31.91	22.71	71%	21.1	3.4%	23 yrs	1.0%
1962	652	36.43	23.30	64%	17.3	3.7%	22 yrs	1.1%
1963	763	41.21	23.41	57%	17.2	3.3%	22 yrs	1.2%
1964	874	46.43	31.24	67%	17.9	3.8%	24 yrs	1.3%
1965	969	53.67	28.61	53%	16.9	3.2%	24 yrs	1.7%
1966	786	57.68	31.89	55%	15.1	3.7%	24 yrs	2.9%
1967	905	53.87	30.19	56%	16.0	3.5%	22 yrs	2.9%
1968	944	57.89	31.34	54%	15.6	3.5%	22 yrs	4.2%
1969	800	57.02	33.90	59%	15.2	3.9%	21 yrs	5.4%
1970	839	51.02	31.53	62%	14.4	4.3%	19 yrs	5.9%
1971	890	55.09	30.86	56%	15.9	3.5%	10 yrs	4.3%
1972	1020	67.11	32.27	48%	14.3	3.4%	20 yrs	3.3%
1973	851	86.17	35.33	41%	10.7	3.8%	20 yrs	6.2%
1974	616	99.04	37.72	38%	7.4	5.1%	17 yrs	11.0%
1975	852	75.66	37.46	50%	10.0	4.9%	16 yrs	9.1%
1976	1005	96.72	41.40	43%	9.7	4.4%	17 yrs	5.8%
1977	831	89.10	45.84	51%	10.1	5.1%	16 yrs	6.5%

SELECTED STATISTICS (CONT.)

	DJIA Close	DJIA Earnings	DJIA Divs	Payout Ratio	Avg. P/E	Div. Yield	Yrs. of Divs at the High	% Chg CPI
1978	805	112.79	48.52	43%	7.3	5.9%	15 yrs	7.6%
1979	839	124.46	50.98	41%	6.8	6.0%	14 yrs	11.3%
1980	964	121.86	54.36	45%	7.2	6.2%	14 yrs	13.5%
1981	875	113.71	56.22	49%	8.1	6.1%	14 yrs	10.3%
1982	1047	9.15	54.14	50%	100.9	5.9%	14 yrs	6.2%
1983	1259	72.45	56.33	78%	16.0	4.9%	14 yrs	3.2%
1984	1212	113.58	60.63	53%	10.4	5.1%	13 yrs	4.3%
1985	1547	96.11	62.03	65%	14.2	4.5%	14 yrs	3.6%
1986	1896	115.59	67.04	58%	15.0	3.9%	16 yrs	1.9%
1987	1939	133.05	71.20	54%	16.4	3.3%	18 yrs	3.6%
1988	2169	215.46	79.53	37%	9.4	3.9%	15 yrs	4.1%
1989	2753	221.48	103.70	47%	11.1	4.2%	17 yrs	4.3%
1990	2634	172.05	102.00	59%	15.6	3.8%	17 yrs	5.8%
1991	3169	49.27	95.18	50%	57.3	3.4%	17 yrs	3.1%
1992	3301	108.25	100.72	50%	30.1	3.1%	17 yrs	2.9%
1993	3754	146.84	99.66	68%	24.0	2.8%	17 yrs	2.7%
1994	3834	256.13	105.66	41%	14.7	2.8%	17 yrs	2.6%
1995	5117	311.02	116.56	37%	14.6	2.6%	19 yrs	2.5%
1996	6448	353.88	131.00	37%	16.7	2.2%	21 yrs	3.3%
1997	——	407.00 e	142.00 e	35%	18.0 e	1.9%	23 yrs	2.3%

50 Yrs
(est. annual growth)
(1946-1996)
6.7%

54% Avg.   13.5 Avg.   4.4% Avg.

The following is a random selection of index and big-cap funds to illustrate how portfolios can vary even though the same company names appear. The top ten stocks in each portfolio can be as low as 10 to 12% of the total portfolio value or as high as 40% or so, even though the company names are essentially identical. The index fund portfolios are, of course, normally very much the same but differ due to the varying times the reports were compiled. Also, the name list and rankings for any given portfolio can shift from one reporting period to another.

INDEX FUNDS

Name	Charge	Approximate Size
Dreyfus S&P 500 Index (800) 645-6561	1.00%	$500mm - $1 billion

Ten Largest Holdings:

General Electric	3.2%
Microsoft	2.5%
Intel	2.4%
Exxon	2.3%
Coca Cola	2.2%
Merck	1.7%
IBM	1.6%
Philip Morris	1.6%
Procter & Gamble	1.4%
WalMart	1.2%

Name	Charge	Approximate Size
Mainstay Instl. Index (800) 695-2126	no load	$500mm - $1 billion

Ten Largest Holdings:

General Electric	3.1%
Microsoft	2.3%
Intel	2.3%
Exxon	2.2%
Coca Cola	2.1%
Royal Dutch	1.6%
Merck	1.6%
IBM	1.6%
Philip Morris	1.5%
Procter & Gamble	1.3%

Vanguard Index Growth   no load $1.5 - $2.0 billion
   (800) 662-7447

Ten Largest Holdings:

General Electric	6.1%
Microsoft	4.5%
Intel	4.3%
Coca Cola	4.2%
Merck	3.1%
Philip Morris	3.1%
Procter & Gamble	2.5%
WalMart	2.3%
Johnson & Johnson	2.1%
Bristol Myers	2.1%

Vanguard Total Stk. Mkt.   no load $4.5 - $5.0 billion
   (800) 662-7447

Ten Largest Holdings:

Coca Cola	1.8%
Microsoft	1.8%
Exxon	1.6%
Intel	1.5%
Merck	1.3%
Philip Morris	1.1%
Procter & Gamble	1.1%
Unocal Corp	1.0%
Johnson & Johnson	0.9%
WalMart	0.8%

Victory Stock Index Fund   4.75% $500mm - $1 billion
   (800) 539-3863

Ten Largest Holdings:

General Electric	3.2%
Microsoft	2.4%
Intel	2.3%
Exxon	2.3%
Coca Cola	2.2%
Merck	1.7%
Royal Dutch	1.6%
Philip Morris	1.6%
IBM	1.6%
WalMart	1.2%

BIG-CAP FUNDS

Name	Charge	Approximate Size
Davis New York Venture	4.75%	$3.5 - $4.0 billion
(800) 279-0279		

Ten Largest Holdings:

IBM	5.0%
Intel	3.9%
American Express	3.6%
Hewlett-Packard	3.4%
Halliburton	3.1%
Travelers Group	2.7%
Philip Morris	2.6%
Masco Corp.	2.3%
Bank of America	2.3%
Citicorp	2.2%

Name	Charge	Approximate Size
Fidelity Dividend Growth	no load	$4.0 - $4.5 billion
(800) 544-8888		

Ten Largest Holdings:

Abbott Labs	5.6%
General Electric	3.8%
Intel	2.8%
Philip Morris	2.3%
Schering Plough	2.2%
Johnson & Johnson	1.8%
Citicorp	1.6%
IBM	1.5%
Bristol Myers	1.4%
Cognizant	1.4%

Name	Charge	Approximate Size
Guardian Stock Fund	6.00%	$2.0 - $2.5 billion
(800) 221-3253 (Annuity)		

Ten Largest Holdings:

General Electric	3.8%
Intel	3.4%
Citicorp	2.5%
Exxon	2.4%
Bristol Myers	2.3%
Johnson & Johnson	2.1%
Philip Morris	2.0%
McDonnell Douglas	1.9%
DuPont	1.9%
Bank of America	1.9%

| MFS Mass. Investors Trust | 5.75% | $4.5 - $5.0 billion |
| (800) 637-2929 | | |

Ten Largest Holdings:

Philip Morris	2.9%
General Electric	2.5%
Colgate Palmolive	2.4%
Norwest	2.4%
Gillette	2.3%
Warner Lambert	2.2%
State Street Corp.	2.1%
Mobil Corp.	1.9%
Progressive	1.8%
McDonnell Douglas	1.8%

| Putnam A Investors Fund | 5.75% | $2.0 - $2.5 billion |
| (800) 225-1581 | | |

Ten Largest Holdings:

General Electric	3.0%
Microsoft	2.8%
Gillette	2.5%
Warner Lambert	2.5%
Intel	2.5%
Pfizer	2.3%
Sears	2.3%
Merck	2.2%
Citicorp	2.1%
Bank of America	2.0%

| United Income A Fund | 5.75% | $6.0 - $6.5 billion |
| (800) 366-5465 | | |

Ten Largest Holdings:

Intel	4.4%
Gillette	2.8%
Caterpillar	2.7%
General Electric	2.6%
Applied Materials	2.6%
DuPont	2.2%
Deere & Co.	1.9%
Cisco Systems	1.8%
Microsoft	1.8%
Air Products	1.5%

Vanguard U.S. Growth Portf.   no load $8.0 - $8.5 billion
    (800) 662-7447

Ten Largest Holdings:

Intel	5.5%
Philip Morris	4.8%
Bristol Myers	4.7%
Monsanto	4.6%
Coca Cola	4.5%
Chase Manhattan	3.6%
Procter & Gamble	3.6%
American Home Products	3.5%
PepsiCo	3.4%
Cisco Systems	3.0%

The following twenty stocks are among the most popular found in today's index funds and big-cap portfolios. The approximate average annual earnings per share growth between 1990 and 1997 (using the author's 1997 estimate at year end) is also shown. All but three (asterisks) are included in the Dow Jones Industrial Average.

American Express	9.6%
AT&T	1.0%
Boeing	2.7%
Bristol Myers *	9.8%
Coca Cola	18.6%
Disney	9.7%
DuPont	11.8%
Exxon	8.8%
General Electric	10.8%
Hewlett-Packard	22.6%
Intel *	39.0%
IBM	2.7%
Johnson & Johnson	16.7%
McDonalds	12.2%
Merck	14.2%
Minnesota Mining	4.9%
Microsoft *	39.3%
Philip Morris	12.8%
Procter & Gamble	11.7%
WalMart	15.7%

The 17 stocks in the Dow are among the fastest growing and averaged about 11.0% annual growth during the seven years. Including the other three, the annual growth averaged 13.7%.

These growth rates should be slowing noticeably in the years ahead.

APPENDIX C

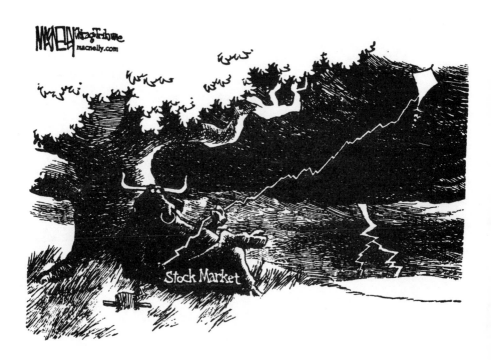

Stock Market

The WALL STREET TRADER software is now available on either 3 1/2" or 5 1/4" discs from Liberty Publishing Company, Inc. The program operates on any IBM or IBM-compatible personal computer with either MS-DOS or WINDOWS. A step-by-step tutorial is also included with each owner's manual.

The data necessary for full operation of The WALL STREET TRADER program can be found every morning in *Investor's Business Daily*, and satisfactory results can also be obtained from data published in *The Wall Street Journal* and elsewhere. Data entry requires no mathematical calculations and about four minutes each day.

To order The WALL STREET TRADER, send $149.95, check or money order, plus $6.00 for shipping and handling to the address below. Or call (800) 251-3345 for immediate 2nd Day Air C.O.D. shipment.

LIBERTY PUBLISHING COMPANY, INC.
440 South Federal Highway, Suite 202
Deerfield Beach, Florida 33441
(954) 360-9000

Order Form

To: **Liberty Publishing Company, Inc.**
440 South Federal Highway, Suite 202
Deerfield Beach, Florida 33441

Gentlemen:

Enclosed is my check or money order for $149.95, plus $6 for shipping and handling. Please send The WALL STREET TRADER software program to the address indicated below. I expect the package to be shipped UPS.

Please ship to...

_____
(Name)

_____
(Street)

_____
(City & Zip)

INDEX